CW01509917

My Dear Kabul

My Dear Kashi

My Dear Kabul

Atifa, Batool, Elahe, Fakhta, Farangis, Farishta, Fatima,
Freshta, Marie, Maryam, Masoma, Mehrsa, Naeema, Najla,
Nilofar, Nora, Parand, Rana, Sadaf, Samira and Zainab

᳅

Translated from Dari and Pashto by
Parwana Fayyaz and Dr Negeen Kargar

Edited by
Parwana Fayyaz, Sunila Galappatti,
Lucy Hannah and Lillie Razvi Toon

CORONET

First published in Great Britain in 2024 by Coronet
An imprint of Hodder & Stoughton Limited
An Hachette UK company

1

A CIP catalogue record for this title is available from the British Library

Hardback ISBN 9781399727983
ebook ISBN 9781399728003

Typeset in Sabon MT by Hewer Text UK Ltd, Edinburgh
Printed and bound in Great Britain by Clays Ltd, Elcograf S.p.A.

Hodder & Stoughton policy is to use papers that are natural, renewable
and recyclable products and made from wood grown in sustainable
forests. The logging and manufacturing processes are expected to
conform to the environmental regulations of the country of origin.

Hodder & Stoughton Limited
Carmelite House
50 Victoria Embankment
London EC4Y 0DZ

www.hodder.co.uk

براى زنان افغانستان

For the women of Afghanistan

د افغانستان د ښځو لپاره

Contents

The making of this book

The editors' introduction

In early 2021, the writers of this collective diary were living in Afghanistan – bar two, who already lived across its borders, in Iran and Tajikistan. They were going to work: among the women were four teachers, a scriptwriter, a lawyer, a doctor, a psychologist, an engineer, an office manager, NGO workers and university students. They were also polishing short stories they had written, due to be collected in an anthology of translated new fiction by Afghan women. The anthology *My Pen Is the Wing of a Bird* (MacLehose Press, 2022) would be many of the writers' first publication. They all belonged to the same writers' group, but few of them had ever met.

Before

Three years before, during a lunch break in a Kabul office, a group of writers told Lucy Hannah (Director, Untold Narratives) that they struggled to get their prose fiction considered for publication. The women writers found it especially difficult to interest local publishers in their work. They longed for opportunities to develop their writing and said they would welcome the support of experienced literary editors and translators, even from outside Afghanistan.

Lucy and the writers began to explore the idea. A call went out for new fiction by women writers living in Afghanistan. Almost two hundred stories arrived, submitted from across the country, many written by hand and photographed on phones or emailed in. A cohort of Afghan readers and translators turned to discussing the submissions, carefully selecting stories to start working with.

A bespoke editorial process was designed. The writers wrote their stories in their own first languages – Dari (Farsi/Persian) and Pashto – with each successive draft translated into English. The logistics of the editorial process were intricate and international: the writers were in Afghanistan, as was Untold's interpreter, Pashtana Durrani. The translators (including Parwana Fayyaz, Dr Negeen Kargar, Margo Munro-Kerr and Dr Zubair Popalzai) were in the UK, as was Untold's team. One editor, Sunila Galappatti, was in Sri Lanka, another, Jacob Ross, temporarily in Grenada. Online calls and messaging were crucial from the outset: after each draft, the writer talked with her translator and editor about developing the story further.

Everyone listened hard. There wasn't the bandwidth for video – it was as much as we could hope that internet connections would last the duration of a call. For some of the writers it was easiest to speak from their workplaces; others preferred cyber cafés in the city. Security was always an issue, electricity was often an issue, but the writers were determined to stay with the process. A year later, another open call went out and the group expanded. This is how the present writers' group was gathered and got to know one another. Meanwhile, the political situation in Afghanistan was precarious and worsening.

With Afghan history, there is always more that came before

Waves of history – competing ancient kingdoms, invasions by successive imperial powers, civil wars – have come and gone in Afghanistan's immutable geography: mountainous, landlocked and positioned at a crossroads between global powers. Najla, the eldest of the writers in this group, was born in 1962, when Afghanistan was already in the midst of political and economic crisis. Within her childhood, Afghanistan's king was deposed by his cousin, brother-in-law and former Prime Minister, Daoud Khan. Daoud declared Afghanistan a republic and himself President of a reforming but autocratic one-party state. Daoud

Khan was then overthrown and brutally assassinated, along with his family, by a Marxist-Leninist party, the People's Democratic Party of Afghanistan. The PDPA began its own programme of reform, land redistribution and violence against its opponents, drawing armed resistance from militant groups across the country. This new government was also riven by internal struggles, and there was another coup. In 1979, the Soviet Union invaded Afghanistan to ensure their preferred faction of the ruling party was installed and stayed in power.

While Najla was at university and starting to work, and while Masoma and Parand were young children, Afghanistan was devastated by civil wars. The Mujahideen, a loose coalition of Islamist militant groups – armed and trained by the US and its regional ally, Pakistan – fought the Soviet troops. When the Soviets were forced to withdraw in 1989, the Mujahideen continued to fight the Afghan government. In the previous decade, since 1978, there had been a dramatic escalation of violence and displacement and a period of persistent conflict had begun.

Many of the writers in this group were born in the 1990s. The Mujahideen were in charge from 1992, but their alliance continued to fracture, with rival groups vying with each other for territory and dominance. Pakistan, with US backing, helped to prop up a faction that might stabilise Afghanistan: it called itself the Taliban, 'the Students'. The Taliban captured Kandahar in 1994, Herat in 1995, and finally took Kabul in late 1996. They took charge of Afghanistan but continued to clash with their rivals. Many of the writers of this book were born to families who had fled the fighting or the new regime to live in neighbouring countries. Meanwhile, the Taliban ruled Afghanistan according to their own unbending interpretation of Islam, highly oppressive to women and girls and ethnic minorities. In 2001, an American invasion toppled the regime, with support from internal and other external forces. An interim administration and then a new republic were established. Many of the writers' families returned to their homeland.

The years that followed were still marred by violence as the presence of the international coalition was resisted by regrouping militants, including the Taliban. There was constant uncertainty and suicide bombings were frequent. Despite this, the writers say that to understand what takes place in their diary, you have to appreciate the reprieve they experienced in the twenty years from 2001 to 2021.

There had been meaningful change, Batool says, and paints a picture of the best of it. Many women had their children in hospitals, with access to healthcare growing. Families encouraged their daughters to go to school, and they left the country's universities as mathematicians, engineers, doctors. They became musicians and learned foreign languages. Safe houses were created for women fleeing domestic abuse; it became possible to make your way out of a forced marriage to a good future. Batool does not for a moment suggest all women had the same access to liberation, but she marvels at a time when both men and women fought for equal rights. Women flew planes and became university professors. Batool laughs as she celebrates that women were powerful even as they were still constrained in many ways. 'Women even judged men's swimming competitions!' she exclaims, describing modestly dressed women with headscarves presiding over men in swimming trunks.

In 2020, the US and the Taliban signed the Doha Accord, following a period of negotiation that side-stepped Afghanistan's elected government. The agreement included provision for the withdrawal of NATO troops and for talks to take place between the Taliban and the Afghan government. The government itself was not party to the agreement. What followed was multi-faceted breakdown and subterfuge. The Taliban stepped up its attacks on Afghan forces and the US stepped down its support for offensive operations by the Afghan military. On the ground, province after province was ceded to the Taliban.

The writers, alongside many of their compatriots, dreaded the country's full return to Taliban control, while there was also disenchantment with the republic across the country and widespread support for a return of the Taliban. In July 2021, Fatima's brother, a soldier in the Afghan national army, was killed in one of the battles for control of Herat, in western Afghanistan. As Parand says in the diary, it was never news the Taliban were coming back, but it still came as a shock. Over a weekend in August, it became clear that the Taliban were on the verge of taking the capital. If Kabul fell, the country would be presumed fallen. When news came that Afghanistan's president had fled the country, the writers found their lives upended, their families under threat, their futures sabotaged.

Asked what Untold Narratives could do for them in these new circumstances, the writers insisted they continue working to meet their anthology deadline and asked Untold if it would also help them stay connected to each other. Initially, Untold held weekly meetings – again WhatsApp audio calls were the platform – to which the writers could come if they wished to talk with others about what they were facing. They came to talk, to listen, to sit in silence. As women were increasingly confined to their homes, one of their worst fears was losing contact with the world outside. They shared these fears in the makeshift refuge of their WhatsApp group. Lucy asked if they would like to continue using the group chat as a place to write about what was happening in their lives.

During

My Dear Kabul is drawn from the messages that were gathered in this way to form a collective diary. Written on the writers' phones, the diary begins as this book does, with Masoma listening to the crows, two days before the fall of Kabul. They kept writing.

Several evenings a week, Untold's then project manager, Will Forrester, downloaded the latest contributions and kept them safe in London so the writers could delete the messages from their own phones. It was safest not to keep a record. Dr Negeen Kargar played the role of both interpreter and translator, helping to set up and frame the forum as a safe space, then producing a translation of the messages from the original Dari and Pashto. She describes the immediate sense of solidarity the diary produced: 'A woman in Kabul would write something and find that a woman in Herat shared her feelings exactly. And here was I, translating in London, feeling the same.'

By the end of the year the translated diary ran close to 200,000 words in all. The writers had written, as one might in a personal diary, when they felt moved to do so. Some, like Najla and Nilofar, wrote consistently through the year; others, like Maryam and Masoma, came and went as life and feeling allowed. There are some writers you can follow through the diary, others whom you can't. More than once, the writers chorus that they are writing the story of living while dead, yet their diary is also full of detailed life and moments of precious relief.

Farangis says it was a place in which she could express her emotions freely – the ones she couldn't share with anyone at home for fear she would make her family more miserable than they were already. For Parand, the diary was initially a place where she could voice her great anger that history was repeating itself. She felt a duty to record the truth of collapse. But in the process of writing, she discovered she was also able to express other, more restorative feelings. For Sadaf, it was simply a relief to gather in a place where 'university girls' like her, often called rebellious or shameless, could own those labels and feel solidarity with each other. Najla points out that, as women, writing was something they *could* do to feel connected to the world while their ties to it were being severed one by one.

Indeed, the writers describe the diary as a kind of safe house.

Najla evokes a home where everyone gathered to tell each other stories. 'Through the diary we felt like everyone was from the same land,' Batool says; the divisions of geography and ethnicity disappeared. Najla agrees: 'No one was a stranger, everyone was related.'

All the same, the writers were conscious of the diary as a record. They often bore silent witness to each other's pain. Everyone was in extremis and they knew they could not make it better, so they tried not to interrupt. Najla says sometimes when she was moved, she expressed private solidarity directly to the writer she'd been reading, instead of adding messages to the group chat. When you read a passage in the diary and are surprised that no one responds to it, these are some of the reasons. So too, the writers remind us, in the midst of turmoil it is not always easy to summon words. Some said they read without writing; others wrote without reading.

Each writer made their submissions in their own first or chosen language – Dari or Pashto. These are the two most widely spoken languages in Afghanistan but not everyone knows both. While all the writers are able to read in Dari, fewer of the group read Pashto fluently – the language in which longer accounts by Najla, Freshta and Naeema appear. In the diary, Farishta, Sadaf and Rana also write in Pashto, although the writers sometimes choose to make their conversational entries in Dari.

Not all contributions were made directly to the group chat group. A few writers – among them Fakhta, Najla, Marie and Zainab – wrote privately in reams and shared their entries with the group at different moments through the year. In this book, those passages are placed in the chronology according to the time they describe rather than the time they were sent in.

Retrospective addition of this kind was especially common with passages that described journeys out of Afghanistan, journeys that were often dangerous and had to be undertaken secretly. We should not play down the security risk that this diary could have posed. It is a testament to the writers' trust in each other that they did share so much within this closed group: they had been brought together as writers and as women; what they knew of each other they learned through the writing they shared.

After

When Batool looks back, she feels they were brave to share incomplete thoughts and inexpressible feelings in the diary. Maryam says that both her sense of time and her feelings of anger have changed since the time she wrote, and she believes the diary helped her become calmer. She says, 'At the time, we used rough words to describe rough feelings.'

No one wrote in the expectation that the diary would become a book, but neither were these accounts written naively. Farangis and Parand said they felt it was an account that would make its way into the world, without imagining how. Atifa and Fatima say they wrote without any sense of a reader, while Zainab insists she chose very consciously what she wanted to express. Freshta looks back on herself: at the time she was writing she felt especially isolated and disconnected from other people. She was in an unfamiliar country and pregnant for the first time, her changing body itself strange to her. She didn't know if her writing made sense to anyone. But then she thought, 'I am writing for the world because the world put us in this situation.'

Parand is adamant, however, that this book is not a plea to the world but something the writers wrote for themselves. They are not asking for rescue but to be seen. As editors, we held fast to this idea that the diary was one the women wrote for themselves and each other. The writers had not granted us – or readers beyond – access to their whole lives, just this fragment of it. The book is a further fragment, approximately 70,000 of the 200,000 or so words originally translated. The writers placed in us an extraordinary trust: we were to edit the book on their behalf, in a language few of them read fluently.

In the early days of editing the diary we talked together about how best to go about our task. We were led by the writers' words first and, barely second, by our translators. Dr Negeen Kargar, herself from Afghanistan, had got to know the writers over two years of working closely with them and being supportive in difficult times. Parwana Fayyaz, also from Afghanistan, shared recent history with the writers; like many of their families, hers had also lived in exile during the first period of Taliban rule, to return hopeful of a new future in the republic. Parwana brought not only her understanding of context but her sensibility and insight as a poet and scholar, guiding us gently through a terrain of language, expression and culture.

Both Negeen and Parwana had worked on the writers' stories as translators, as Sunila Galappatti had as an editor. Sunila has never been to Afghanistan. But in the fractured feelings and spirited resistance expressed in the diary, she heard echoes of other perpetual conflicts, and striking parallels with women recounting war in Sri Lanka, where she comes from. Lillie Razvi Toon came from a background in human rights and international law, a perspective that informed her approach to the work. Lucy Hannah carried a detailed history of conversation and connection with the writers. Lucy had remained alongside the diary from the moment it was suggested, and it was her conviction that this diary should become a book.

A close team of insiders and outsiders, we sat together to talk about our reading of the original diary and the book we imagined coming out of it. The principles were not difficult to agree: we wanted to honour the individual voices and also the collective chorus, keeping the group together. We wanted to avoid editorial explanation, believing that our work was to lead readers into the women's world, not to simplify it for the reader. In the diary, you find the everyday mess of conflict: news is never certain, there are differing reports, contradictory truths. We did not try to render the writers' world more logical than it is.

We stopped much longer to talk about structure. How should the material be arranged? We explored options before returning to our first instinct: it was a diary written in real time and should be presented chronologically. As a rule, we allowed ourselves little poetic licence with the chronology. There is some taken here and there to ease the flow of the edited manuscript, but, overall, we held to the feeling that each passage was written in context and spoke for a specific moment.

We wanted to let the silences in the book remain. The diary does not show you everything that happened in Afghanistan that year – far from it. The writers' priority beyond describing their situation was living through it. If they mention one incident but don't speak of another, that distinction may not be especially significant. But they are clear about this: in a society divided along geographical, historical, ethnic, religious, gendered and countless other lines, nothing and no one is unaffected by conflict. They reminded us they were women writing about a situation that has also been devastating for men.

The manuscript went through many rounds of editing before we were sure of its shape – it seemed the only way to distil the original diary was to go gently, peeling back layer after layer until we could see a form emerge. The translation also remained dynamic, Parwana retracing the Dari as we worked, Negeen refining the passages in Pashto. Needless to say, we had to remain responsive to the fluctuating security situation in Afghanistan, up to the last minute. In the book you are reading, some names have been changed, surnames removed and some details excised. These were decisions we made in consultation with the writers, and regretfully, aware that in prioritising their safety, we were rendering some aspects of their lives invisible.

Calls with the writers were a regular feature of the process, from start to finish. Sometimes we all spoke together, sometimes in small groups or with one writer at a time. These calls were to hear their wishes for the book, their worries about it, and other details from their lives that informed their words. Parwana described each season of the edited manuscript in recorded voice notes and Negeen did the same in writing, so the writers could tell us if we were on the right track. We did this because of what we didn't do, which was to rebuild the edited manuscript in the original languages. It is important that you know this: the writers didn't get to read the manuscript in full before it was submitted for publication. So, this book is underscored by trust: as they trusted each other in the writing of the diary, they have trusted us to edit it into a book. We wish to express our deep gratitude for that grace.

We hoped ultimately to produce a book that spoke to Afghan readers even as it did to readers elsewhere, never making a choice between them. We believed it was equally a book for readers who know nothing about Afghanistan as for readers who know everything; a book that could startle those who have never known war and offer solidarity to those who have. As Farangis says, history has not stopped repeating. Indeed, Masoma asks the most testing question of all: 'What will this book change? Are we just throwing it out into the night?'

January 2024

About the writers

2021, before the book begins

Atifa

Atifa is a 24-year-old activist and aid worker. She was born in Bamyan, in mountainous central Afghanistan, but her family moved to the city of Herat in western Afghanistan a few years later. Atifa studied at Herat University of Education and graduated in 2019. She works for an organisation that offers free English classes to young girls and boys, and helps older women learn to read and write. She lives with her mother, sisters and youngest brother; her father has just died from an illness.

Batool

Batool, now 35, was born in Damascus in 1986. She and her family were migrants from Afghanistan. For as long as she can remember, they were always leaving. The family lived briefly in Lebanon, but Syria was the place to which they kept returning. When conflict began to take hold in Syria, Batool's family fled to Turkey and through the mountains to Isfahan in Iran, where she became a psychologist and university teacher. While in Isfahan, she married. Batool had known her husband since childhood; his family were also migrants from Afghanistan. They had three children: a boy and two girls. After the first fall of the Taliban, Batool's husband began working back in Afghanistan and Batool eventually decided to join him there with the children, despite his concerns that it was not the right place for her. In Kabul, she teaches Psychology at the university and works as a mental health therapist, journalist and women's rights activist, while finishing a PhD at a university in

Iran. She writes fiction because 'it is a powerful weapon that can give voice to women who have no means to scream'.

Elahe

Elahe's parents fled the violence in Afghanistan with her older brother and sister in 1980, ten years before Elahe – now 31 – was born. They wanted their children to be safe, with the chance of an education and a better life. Elahe grew up with her mother's bitter-sweet stories of life in Kabul when she was young and Elahe's father worked for Kabul Bank, delivering letters on his old English bicycle. In Iran, Elahe's parents both had agricultural jobs and the family lived in a village outside Tehran. It was an hour's walk to and from school, but Elahe managed to complete her education. She went to university in a different province, after the Iranian government relaxed some of its restrictions on refugees. After graduating, she taught computer skills to the children of undocumented Afghan migrants. Elahe has worked on and off – in an office, in a trouser factory – but for refugees in Iran it is not easy to find work, or to work for fair pay. Elahe dreams of returning to live and work in Afghanistan. She has never been there.

Fakhta

Fakhta was only six months old when her family left Afghanistan for Pakistan in 1999, then moved on to Iran. They left because of the dangers posed by the Taliban during their first regime (1996–2001). When the Taliban was toppled, Fakhta's father decided to take his family back home to Daikundi, in the mountains of central Afghanistan. Fakhta is now in her final year studying Law at university in Kabul, living in student accommodation. She is 22 and planning her wedding.

Farangis

Farangis, 29, is a lawyer with her own practice. She also works with a legal organisation that offers training to different departments of the state legislature and builds the capacity of women to access the law. She describes herself as a lawyer by profession and a writer by passion. Farangis and her husband are about to board a charter flight at the insistence of their families, a week before her first child is due. They have lived in America before and have US green cards, which allow them to be evacuated early when it becomes clear the Taliban are about to take Kabul.

Farishta

Farishta, 27, was born in Ghazni, Afghanistan but spent her early childhood in Pakistan. The family went into exile for their safety during the first Taliban takeover of Afghanistan, because her father had held a position in the previous government. One day when she was little, she came home singing a familiar Pakistani nursery rhyme that proclaims a love for Pakistan. Her father was shocked and encouraged her to sing the same rhyme replacing Pakistan with Afghanistan, her original homeland. He encouraged his daughters to grow up patriotic, powerful and expecting to work. Farishta is currently working with a project that supports children in rural areas who have missed out on education due to conflict. She and her sisters live with their mother in Kabul; their father died four years ago.

Fatima

Fatima, 23, was born on the first day of spring, Nowruz, in 1998. She lives with her family in the city of Herat. Fatima is due to begin the final semester of her degree in English Language and Literature at Herat University. Her mother and sister encourage her to write, as do her friends, Fatima says, but society struggles to tolerate a woman with an opinion and a pen. Fatima's brother, a soldier in the Afghan national army, was killed in combat just weeks ago, in the efforts to prevent Taliban capture of his hometown.

Freshta

Freshta is 24. She was born in Kunar Province, near the Afghan–Pakistani border, but grew up in Kabul. She wrote her first stories as a schoolgirl and published them under a pen name because she knew her parents would disapprove. She studied Law and Political Science at university and worked as a journalist. She fled the country in 2019, when the Taliban threatened the radio station where she worked as a reporter of women's affairs. With her husband, she crossed the border into neighbouring Tajikistan. Freshta has not been able to find work in Tajikistan and is now expecting her first child.

Marie

Marie, 29, was born in Kabul but her family left for Quetta, Pakistan when she was three years old, and she only knew Afghanistan through her mother's stories. It was a beautiful picture her mother painted, especially of Kabul River. A young teenager when the family moved back to Afghanistan after the establishment of the Islamic Republic, Marie was surprised to find the city less poetic than she expected. She studied for her first degree at Kabul University's Faculty of Psychology and Educational Sciences, then went to India to complete a master's degree. She worked for NGOs in Kabul while making real a dream she and a friend had, to establish a women-run counselling service. She works from 8 a.m. to 4 p.m. at her day job and 4 p.m. to 8 p.m. and weekends in her own office at the Meaning of Life.

Maryam

Maryam is 25; her early childhood was dominated by the first Taliban takeover of Afghanistan. When that government fell and schools and universities reopened for girls, she was able to go to school and then study Law at the University of Kabul. But as a life-long health condition worsened, Maryam became increasingly wheelchair bound and unable to work. She and her siblings live together, with their parents, in their childhood home in Kabul. From Maryam's bedroom window she can touch the leaves of the quince tree that grows just beneath it. She and the tree grew up together.

Masoma

Masoma, 47, says, 'It's easy to lose your way when you reflect that nothing you write will change society – but maybe what we write is the beginning of a tree, and its fruits will ripen years later.' Masoma was born in Iran in 1974 and moved between Afghanistan and Iran with successive political developments: the Soviet occupation of Afghanistan and the first rule of the Taliban. Masoma was studying engineering at university in Mazar-e-Sharif, one of three girls out of seventy-five students on the course, when her education was disrupted by the first Taliban takeover. After the Taliban left, she finished her degree and worked as a draughtswoman for construction companies, though her work was confined to the office; as a woman she was not allowed to be a site engineer. She hasn't been able to work for a few years because she looks after her mother, who has Alzheimer's.

Mehrsa

Mehrsa, 29, is from Bamyan Province. Born as refugees in Iran, she and her five siblings had to work as children to help their family earn a living, and their early education was in informal camp settings. Moving back to Afghanistan aged twelve, from a very flat part of Iran, Mehrsa was fascinated that houses were built on the sides of mountains. Mehrsa's father was not willing to pay for his daughters' education beyond a point in secondary school, but Mehrsa persisted with hers, winning scholarships and helped by her older sister, who was working. She was eventually able to go to a school in Kabul that encouraged girls to believe in themselves. She went on to university in Bangladesh. Mehrsa's family lived in Kabul but would travel back to Bamyan, the landscape that inspires her writing, with its lakes and apricot trees and ancient lore. Mehrsa won a Fulbright scholarship to do a master's in Women's and Gender Studies at a university in Cedar Falls, Iowa, USA. She has just left Afghanistan, her joy at beginning her course suddenly extinguished by the prospect she might never return home.

Naeema

Naeema, 36, was born in Wardak Province, famous for its gardens and apples. The family moved between Kabul and Wardak, depending on which was safer at any given time. It was challenging at times to leave Kabul's amenities for rural austerity, but the mountainous landscapes of Wardak are, Naeema believes, what made her a writer. Naeema went to Kabul University and is active in cultural groups in the city. She is part of another writing group and is the director of a foundation that has published more than sixty books for children. What troubles her is that you never know if a story will reach the people it needs to reach.

Najla

Najla, 58, was born in Kabul in 1962. Her father died when she was eleven years old, but the family fulfilled his wish that all of his children be educated. While in university, studying Language and Literature, she worked part-time in a government job to support her family. She was given housing by the Soviet-backed state, in which she still lives. Najla met her husband at work. Her stories are based on the ordinary people she meets; she feels if she isn't in contact with people, she can't write. The eldest of the group, she has seen forty-three years of war, as she puts it, and has been writing as long. Her early notebooks were lost during a period of exile, but she has kept everything since. Najla has five children and seven grandchildren.

Nilofar

Nilofar, 33, is from Mazar-e-Sharif, in northern Afghanistan, but spent much of her childhood as a refugee in Iran. Her parents also died in Iran, when she was five. Six months after 9/11, when the Taliban were overthrown, Nilofar returned to Afghanistan in the care of her older siblings. She was then thirteen, the second youngest in the family. She had gone to school in Iran but in Afghanistan her older brothers would not let her go to school. Once they were married and living separate lives, Nilofar returned to school (at the age of twenty-three) and went on to study Political Science at university before starting on a second degree in Literature. She works for projects supporting vulnerable people and is in the final year of her Literature degree. She lives with a brother and sister.

Nora

Nora, 27, grew up in Kabul. Her early childhood was during the Taliban's first rule, so she and her siblings were educated at home until the Taliban departed. She says her home was like a school, with six children encouraged to prepare each time any one of them had a test. Nora loved literature but her mother wanted her to become a doctor, so she went to medical school. She got married in her final year of study and postponed her specialisation as a gynaecologist to take maternity leave. She has two children, aged six and one, and is now back working as a doctor. On 14 August, the night before the Taliban enters Kabul, she is working the night shift in the hospital.

Parand

Parand, 39, is a scriptwriter who loves her work. She began to have confidence in herself as a writer after she showed a story to Najla and Najla thought it was good. Parand and Najla are firm friends. Parand spends her time between Kabul and Kunduz

Province. She is a voracious reader, a lover of landscape and finds joy in little things.

Rana

Rana, 27, is a teacher. She was born in Pakistan, where her father would tell his children how beautiful their homeland was. When she was eight, they returned excitedly to Afghanistan after the first fall of the Taliban, only to discover their old house had been badly damaged in the fighting. Her father set about rebuilding it and restoring the garden he'd loved. Rana watched him build the house and came to love it as fiercely. She wanted to become a doctor but didn't get into medical school, so her father encouraged her to study Pashto Literature instead, which she did at Kabul University. Rana's father retired early from the military and would bring home books of all kinds. During power outages, the family would gather around while he read to them by candlelight. Rana's whole family encourages her to write.

Sadaf

Sadaf, 26, grew up in Kabul, the eldest of her siblings. She describes her life as being built on a happy, free childhood in which, until the age of fifteen, she played outdoors. She studied Literature at Kabul University and has recently begun working as a schoolteacher.

Samira

Samira, 28, was born in Ghazni Province, south of Kabul. The eldest of five children, she is in the capital, studying Persian Literature at Kabul University. She says she feels luckier than many women, to have had a father who encouraged her to speak freely and respect herself. Samira is married; her husband is currently living and working in France.

This map shows the provinces and cities
referred to by the writers

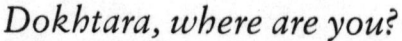

Dokhtara, where are you?

It has been cloudy almost every morning. The cawing of crows fills the air. In the old days, when we heard that sound, my mother would say, 'Good news, good news, I will give you honey and milk,' and then she would wait days to hear news from her people, who lived far away. I don't remember if she ever received this news or not. But I read bad news every day I hear these crows.

Herat fell today. Ghazni fell yesterday. Sar-e-pol, Sheberghan, Spin Boldak, Malestan, the previous days. It's like a game of dominoes. I don't know where this will stop or who will have the ability to stop it.

Masoma, 13 August 2021

I
Kabul falls
15–19 August 2021

15 August 2021

Maryam, 11:33:57, Kabul
Dokhtara, girls, are you okay? Please let us know
how you are doing?

I am worried.

I am at home.

The internet is very bad.

> **Nora, 11:34:30, Kabul**
> Everywhere we turn there is bad news. Nothing
> can stop the Taliban from reaching Kabul now.
>
> Is everyone trying to run away from here? Where
> is everyone going?

Nilofar, 11:38:46, Mazar-e-Sharif
The Taliban have entered our area of Mazar.
They've met with the local elders and told them,
'We won't do anything to you. Go about your lives.
Women just need to follow the rules of hijab.'

> **Samira, 11:39:17, Kabul**
> They are lying. They said the same thing in
> Herat.

Samira, 11:40:01

Now the Taliban have entered the Barchi area.*

Maryam, 11:40:21

Oh God, this means they're here in Kabul?

Nilofar, 11:46:24

Even in Mazar, they entered the city so quietly.
Everyone is worried this is the calm before the storm.

Fatima, 11:51:09, Herat

In the first days, they remain calm. As time
passes, they will start to inflict their inhumane
laws on innocent people.

Maryam, 11:51:51

In Herat, they banned women from going to
university.

Fatima, 11:52:25

Yes, they closed the universities in our faces.
They locked young girls out of schools.

Maryam, 11:52:44

As of now, they've evacuated Kabul University.

Nilofar, 11:53:06

Has Kabul fallen?

---

*Dasht-e-Barchi is in western Kabul. The area's residents are mostly from
the Hazara community, and it has previously been targeted for attack by
the Taliban and other extremist militias. Recent sites of suicide bombings
in Barchi include schools and a maternity hospital.

Maryam, 11:53:13

No.

But they've just entered.

The clash has begun.

Some people have locked themselves in their offices.

Fatima, 11:53:54

They've beaten some girls in the alleys for not
wearing the right kind of hijab.

Maryam, 11:54:10

Where are you?

Fatima, 11:53:54

We are in Herat.

Maryam, 12:02:11

Dokhtara, don't you think we are under threat?
The Taliban have warned the famous poet
Samay Hamed. So, it seems they are after
writers and social activists. I am scared for the
day they cut off our internet and we lose contact
with the world. How are we going to
communicate?

Fatima, 12:06:07

I am really scared. The Taliban have started
searching houses. And we have army uniforms
around the house.

Fatima, 12:07:06

Our heads are under an axe.

> **Samira, 12:07:03**
> Don't be afraid, I think they are only going to search houses reported to have weapons. They also search the houses of army officers and government workers. I heard they searched the house of the Attorney General and left a mess.

> **Samira, 12:07:28**
> They had shouted out to bring forward any weapons.

Maryam, 12:07:34

I am scared on account of our *ketabha*, books.

> **Samira, 12:07:35**
> They stayed around the house for a few days.

Maryam, 12:07:44

They might either take them or burn them.

> **Samira, 12:07:46**
> They didn't do anything to my family.

> **Samira, 12:07:54**
> As of now, they haven't done anything to books either.

Maryam, 12:08:44

So, what do they come for?

Maryam, 12:08:50

Nothing is known yet.

Maryam, 12:10:14

I am sorry about my erratic messages.

> **Marie, 12:11:19, Kabul**
>
> I was very scared today. It usually takes me an hour to get home to Barchi from Shahr-e-Naw.*
> Today, it took me six hours.

> **Marie, 12:11:48**
>
> Every time I saw the Taliban passing by in their cars, I thought they were going to shoot us.

Sadaf, 12:17:58, Kabul

Salam, everyone.

Yes, they have entered Kabul.

We all left our universities and offices and returned home in fear.

> **Fatima, 12:19:54**
>
> I'm scared too. My brother was martyred as a soldier. My parents work on military bases. My sister is also training with the military.

Maryam, 12:23:17

Please be careful, all of you.

---

*Shahr-e-Naw, meaning 'new town', is in central Kabul. The writers often use it as a point of orientation, to evoke the centre of town. Ansari round-about is another central landmark often mentioned, located in Shahr-e-Naw.

Batool, 12:24:36, Kabul

Dokhtara, whoever among you is currently living in Kabul, please stay safe and keep calm. There won't be any shooting. Stay inside and don't go outside unless you have to. If you're panicking, it will only bring turbulence to your surroundings.

They won't cause unrest in the city. There will be a negotiation in the presidential palace and the media will announce the result.

Sadaf, 12:25:56

Yes, that's right. I also believe these are all rumours we hear. They've only entered Kabul. No one has heard of any shooting yet.

Maryam, 12:28:14

Batool jan, the president has already resigned. Rumour has it they will announce that today. My only fear is the Taliban break their promise and take the presidential palace with their fighters.

Maryam, 12:29:15

I just hope they won't do anything to people and their homes.

Batool, 12:30:36

Nothing will happen, *azizam*, my dear. We are witnessing a transition period, exactly as planned. The Taliban are supposed to take over temporarily. We must not lose hope. Let's stay very strong, especially in this age of propaganda and fake news.

Maryam, 12:30:38

If there is nothing serious to worry about,
why have they disrupted the telecom
networks?

Sadaf, 12:32:35

I don't know who sold this country again.
But I saw that someone named its price.

Maryam, 12:33:33

Yes, Sadaf jan, our people have paid the price of
war.

Marie, 12:34:25

Batool jan, no matter what phase of the war we
found ourselves in, no matter what position we
took, every time, the people paid its price. The
barbaric Taliban won't follow any rules.

Sadaf, 12:40:08

Unfortunately.

Freshta, 13:30:00, Dushanbe, Tajikistan

I have my mobile in my hand and watch this
cruel show that technology records all day long.
It begins to stick to my memories. I don't know
which pain to write about. My fingers can't
move on the keyboard.

Maryam, 15:00:00

My hands cannot write either. My notebook and
my books are at the window – they wonder why
I am not writing. Perhaps my notebook knows I

have no words in my heart to share with it. I
cannot tell it that the Taliban have reached the
gates of this city.

*A long day progresses into evening. Time and again the writers
check where everyone is, and what the news is.*

Nilofar, 16:23:49

Azizan-e-Kabul, dear Kabul-dwellers, I hope you
are staying safe.

> **Atifa, 16:26:14, Herat**
>
> Where are you??

Nilofar, 16:26:16

In Mazar-e-Sharif. This morning the Taliban
had a meeting in our area. They were walking
around so freely. The people were in shock.

> > **Fatima, 21:10:56**
> >
> > And now our great and beautiful Kabul has
> > fallen into the hands of these wild animals. Our
> > people are going to be killed.
> >
> > **Fatima, 21:10:58**
> >
> > Our president sold our country and escaped.

Nora, 21:18:23, Kabul

I don't know how to express my feelings. It
seems that for years, Kabul has been guarded by
a shepherd who was with the wolf. They left the
city and its children in the hands of these wild
men.

Marie, 20:19:00

Whenever I hear any sound that is loud like gunfire, my heart stops. I fear the Taliban will start their search of homes tonight. And my family will pay the price for my working with foreigners. This is the first time I wish I lived in the furthest reaches of Kabul.

Fatima, 21:10:42

I cannot breathe.

Maryam, 03:22:00

I don't have any sleep. It is night-time, and
Kabul has fallen fully. I cannot believe it. I want
to tell everyone: they took Kabul. I want to tell
my mother, my sisters, my brothers – they have
taken Kabul. I want to go up to the roof and
say quietly – they took Kabul. I don't know
why I can't just shout it out: THEY TOOK
KABUL.

&

Through the night and into the next morning the writers reflect on what has happened and recount the day they have just lived through.

Fakhta, Kabul

Fakhta lives in a university hostel in the capital, and is close to getting her degree in Law from Kabul University. Her home is in the mountainous province of Daikundi.

I woke up when my phone rang. My mother gave me the news. She said our whole province – including our district, Nili, at the centre of Daikundi – is in the hands of the Taliban. She was upset. She said, 'I wish you had not gone back to the university in Kabul.'

She was right. Apart from Kabul, all other cities are already in the hands of the Taliban. They now control all the highways. The only thing left to happen was for the Taliban to enter the capital and take over the presidential palace. I said goodbye to my mother and lay back on my bed in the hostel, looking out of the window, shocked and anxious.

I got up and went to class. I was late and slipped into the lecture. After about twenty minutes, everyone's phone began to ring; the lecturer's too.

Sadaf

Sadaf is a teacher. She is teaching a class of girls in Year 8, most of whom would be fourteen or fifteen years old.

I distributed the exam papers and gave my students their instructions. At 11 a.m.

I explained the instructions to them and wrote a few more on the blackboard with white chalk. The students asked questions and I answered them. The class was so calm, like the silence before a storm. Then the door opened, and the head teacher came in. She started collecting the exam papers although we hadn't even started. Her hands were shaking, and she asked me to help her. I saw my students' faces, pale with fear. We told them to go home.

Parand, Kabul

Parand is a scriptwriter and has been working with the same colleagues for several years.

I was at the office, as usual. I had only just started working when the phone rang. We were told that the situation was getting worse, that the Taliban had entered the city and we should leave the office. I was not afraid: it was not news. We knew the Taliban would be coming back and I witnessed the same turmoil twenty-five years ago. But I had no choice but to leave alongside two of my colleagues, who were younger and so afraid you could see their skin turn pale.

Fakhta

As I walked quickly back to the university hostel, I worried about my fiancé. He is in the army in Uruzgan Province. He is someone who has fought the Taliban face to face. If he is recognised by any of them, I will have to say goodbye forever. I knew he was in Kabul for a few days, on leave, and all the way back to the hostel I kept trying to reach him on my phone. I must have called twenty times. But I never got to hear his voice.

Hurrying my steps, I ran into the hostel grounds. As I entered the corridor, everyone was leaving, some with luggage, some with belongings stuffed into plastic bags. In my room, I saw Mitra gathering her things. Without saying Salam, she told me to collect my stuff and leave the hostel as soon as possible. 'The teachers said it is only for a few days. When the situation gets better, we can come back.' I said goodbye to Mitra and picked up a plastic bag. I put in a few clothes and *Kafka on The Shore*. I was reaching for my ID card and other documents which I keep at the back of my bookshelf when the teacher in charge shouted at me to leave so she could close the hostel.

Najla, Kabul

Najla works as an office manager but is not at work on 15 August.

We needed money at home. The way to the bank was long; I had to pass through the market. Men and women were busy shopping for their daily groceries. For a moment, I felt happy that life was going on. I saw a few people I pass daily, who used to shave their beards and now have left them to grow. I saw high-school girls. I enjoyed looking at them in their black uniforms with white headscarves. I asked myself if I would see this sight again. When I arrived at the bank, there was such a huge crowd I thought there must be a protest. People were shouting and swearing at the bank staff. Police were trying to bring some order to the crowd.

Sadaf

It was crowded in the streets. No one could pass through, neither pedestrians nor cyclists. Everyone was in shock and panicking. The roads were blocked. I decided to take the longer route home, around the back of the mountain. At this moment, I saw my brother coming in his car to pick me up and drop me home safely. I was scared, but not as scared as we were before Karzai's government.* I also lived five years in such chaos. Maybe we are used to it. The only thing that upsets me is this: as a child I grew up in wartime, as a young girl I saw war; when will I be able to live?

Fakhta

Everyone was running towards the main road. I joined a couple of girls heading in that direction. Around me, I could only see girls with luggage trying to hail taxis. Because of the demand, taxis charged three or four times the usual amount.

---

*Hamid Karzai was initially appointed interim head of a transitional administration after the US and its allied forces overthrew the Taliban in 2001. He was then elected president of the new Islamic Republic of Afghanistan in 2004. 'Karzai's government' is used repeatedly in the writers' diary as a shorthand marker of a change of regime, culture and the departure of the Taliban.

One of the girls asked me where I wanted to go. The question hit me hard. I didn't know. My only place in Kabul was the hostel. I have some distant relatives in Kabul who are poor, and I didn't want to be a burden on them. I tried calling my fiancé again. Maybe he had relatives I could go to in Kabul. But I couldn't reach him though I tried five or six times. A vehicle came, heading for Barchi. The girls with me wanted to go to Barchi. Afraid of being left alone, I said I would also go to Barchi. All the way, I kept trying to reach my fiancé, but I could not speak to him.

Parand

The driver sped through the streets. We were lucky not to see any of the Taliban, but the panic around us was overwhelming. Everyone was running in different directions. We were also driven in an unknown direction through the crowd. Finally, we found ourselves in Char-rahi Baraki.

Next to our office car was a taxi, also trying to get somewhere. A man leaned out of it and said to our driver, 'Brother, leave the car and save yourself. I left my office car in the middle of the road and took this taxi.' At the same time, our driver got a call advising him to leave us on the road and return the car to the office. I was shocked to see this sudden change in men. For them, the car was more valuable than three women's lives in the midst of this horror.

Najla

I was scared. I abandoned my trip to the bank and started back for home. I had to pass through the market again – now women were even running away. In the blink of an eye, the shopkeepers closed their shops. I heard that the Taliban had crossed Pul-e-Charkhi prison in Kabul and were coming into the city. It was said they had entered the city from all possible sides, broken the prison doors and set all prisoners free. A few men passed on motorbikes, with long unkempt hair and guns in hand. The things I usually saw on TV, I now saw in front of me. There was gunfire and I thought war had started. Suddenly, I saw many aeroplanes in the sky.

Marie

Marie is approaching her thirtieth birthday, working in the marketing department of a German aid agency in Kabul and heading her own organisation, a women-led counselling service, in her spare time. She lives with her parents and siblings.

We were told to work from home. I collected my laptop charger from the office and quickly took the road to Ansari roundabout. The roundabout was unbearably crowded. I saw people rushing, trying to get somewhere, all tangled up in each other. Every person looked unhappy: they swore if their way was blocked. There were no traffic police. It was not normal at all.

After a lot of trouble, I found a taxi with four women and a man. The man sat in the front seat. He said to the taxi driver, 'Hurry up, please, the Taliban has reached Shahrak Ettefaq.' I asked, 'Where is Shahrak Ettefaq?' He answered, 'Dasht-e-Barchi.' It was not just me: the other three women also froze in their seats.

Parand

We had to walk amid the moving crowd. There were a few men who laughed at us, saying, *At last your good times are gone; now you women will have to stay inside.* A few were enjoying themselves so much they hurled abuse at us – in words, and then physically. We walked for two hours before I saw a member of my family – my eyes welled up at the sight of them. Since then, I've been wondering, is it just the Taliban or all men in this country who are against women's freedom?

Najla

Back at home, I listened to the news: the Taliban had taken over Kabul, and Ashraf Ghani* left the country with his staff. The Taliban were in the presidential palace.

What will happen tomorrow?

---

*Ashraf Ghani, president of Afghanistan, fled Kabul by helicopter in the early afternoon of 15 August 2021, a vivid symbol of surrender amid uncertainty about what had or had not taken place. The Taliban entered the presidential palace unopposed.

Marie

After two hours of driving, finally, I could see the yellow Silo building* behind the trees. I had to walk the rest of the way home. I was very close to Kot-e-Sangi† when I heard people rushing, calling to each other that the Taliban had reached District 5. I imagined the Taliban with their whips in hand, running after people and beating us to our death. The way I was dressed could be dangerous: they would shoot me right away, I thought. I started running too. My throat was dry and burning with fear. My feet started to give up on me, I kept losing my balance.

Yesterday's city had disappeared. The shops were closed. The men with their fruit and vegetable carts were gone. Kot-e-Sangi, which could always contain human after human, had emptied out completely. Even the sun did not feel like yesterday. Everywhere felt dark and full of fright.

It was as though the people of this city had died before the Taliban entered Kabul. These dead people were now carrying their bodies in search of a graveyard in which to rest. On Sunday, 15 August 2021, the city of Kabul and its people turned into a Miyazaki animation.

---

*The Silo building is another landmark of Kabul, a Soviet-built grain silo and bread factory that has more recently served as a military base and prison.
†Kot-e-Sangi is one of Kabul's more populated areas, a settlement on a rocky hillside that rises in the west of the city.

Sadaf

As it grew dark, our hearts also darkened. Today the streets of our neighbourhood were empty in the evening. No children playing, nobody buying groceries, no students with rucksacks on their backs gathering to socialise below our block. We moved uncertain, like ghosts. At dinner, the children of our family looked frightened with every bite they took. To calm our anxiety, we went to bed and turned off the lights. I covered my eyes with my headscarf to shield my mind from the pain of the world. But the pain had already made its home in my thoughts. I don't know when my eyes closed, but I woke to gunfire around 3 a.m. I thought they had attacked our street – but then the firing calmed down. I couldn't hear the birds singing. Maybe they were also scared or maybe they were quiet to respect our grief.

ಲ

The next day, 16 August 2021

Najla

No one comes out of their homes; the whole city is quiet. A few days ago, there were so many dogs in the streets of Kabul, who would bark the whole night. Even those dogs are silent now. At 10.30 last night, I heard a big explosion far from our home. I was scared. I listened to the Taliban's loudspeaker announcements: they asked civilians not to come out of our homes.

In the morning, I heard the azaan, the call to prayer, from the mosque loudspeakers. As usual, I prayed and tried to listen to the birds singing. But I could not hear them. Maybe you won't believe me, but this is true.

At 6 a.m. I looked out of the window. I saw dogs but they were not barking, as if they were scared too. I hid behind the curtains. I saw the Taliban walking on the streets. They were pointing and shouting, *Search him, search him*. I can no longer hear many aeroplanes in the sky. Maybe everyone left yesterday.

ॐ

Maryam

Salam *dost-ha*. Greetings, friends.

Maryam

I hope you're online.

Atifa

Salam, Maryam. Yes, I am here.

> **Maryam**
>
> The Taliban have started interrogating households.
>
> **Maryam**
>
> If you have any documents, hide them.

Atifa

Where? Which province? Kabul?

> **Maryam**
>
> Or just destroy them.
> In Kabul, yes.

Batool

Are you sure, azizam?

> **Maryam**
>
> Yes, very sure.

Parand

Not yet, though?

> **Maryam**
>
> Yes, they have started. In Kart-e-Char and
> Shahrak Haji Nabi.
>
> **Maryam**
>
> Girls are asking what to do.

Atifa

Oh my God. I hope things turn for the good.

> ### Batool
>
> Thank you, Maryam jan, for letting us know. Although I think home-searching has not begun in Shahrak yet? But we have received some messages to hide our documents or send them elsewhere to be safe.

Maryam

You can never trust the Taliban. They won't make any official announcement of their plans. We can see with our own eyes their flag waving everywhere in the alleys. Yet the news says nothing about their arrival in the city. The news lies.

> ### Batool
>
> Yes, *junam*, my dear, we cannot trust the Taliban. These days I don't even trust my neighbours.

Nora

On the morning of 15 August, Nora had just come off the night shift from her job as a doctor in a maternity hospital. She thought the panic on the streets must be due to the fall of other provinces to the Taliban, never believing they had entered Kabul. She followed her plan to go to the gym on her way home and only there did she realise what had happened. She was in gym clothes, with nothing to cover her head or comply with the Taliban codes of dress for women. It took her two hours to drive home though she didn't live far away. When she arrived, her six-year-old son asked her to put on traditional clothes so they wouldn't be killed by the Taliban.

There is a strange silence that surrounds us.
There is no sound of children crying, nor of
vendors offering fresh vegetables for ten Afghani.
Not even the sound of cars crowding the city. I
miss the city of Kabul: that sound of life and
survival. I even miss the kids who used to play
across our corridor, screaming their hearts out. I
live in the most crowded part of Kabul, in Kart-
e-Char, but today it has the dreadful silence of a
grave. This is a silence that does not bring calm
but madness. It has swallowed the entire city, it
will slowly swallow me too.

Marie

I hide in my room like a moving corpse, thinking
about a future that never existed.

I read the news, and I think about the girls and
women of my country. How will they live after
this? How hard they tried to live a decent life. In
a moment, their efforts were snatched away.
Now that I look back, it seems all this time we
were circus slaves, at the hands of a master who
managed to vanish from the stage like a skilled
magician. What humiliation.

Maryam

I have a headache from looking at my phone all day.
What has happened? What could happen? Why this
way? Why that way? I have gone mad. Give me
more news. I have no appetite but only nausea.
News, news, news. Headache, headache, headache.
America. Aeroplane. Taliban. Migration. Control.
Kabul Air Traffic. America. Women.

America has announced that a Taliban
government will only be recognised if they
respect basic human rights. I lose my reasoning
even trying to understand what that means.
What are our rights? To survive and that is all?
The Taliban won't even let us choose what to
wear, they've already made an announcement
about that.

Marie

Since yesterday I haven't eaten anything. I don't
feel hungry at all. Everyone is feeling like this. My
mother asks me, 'What shall I cook for dinner?'
Maybe she believes this horror can be dispelled
with food. I don't answer her. I am too tired even
to offer her a few words. Words make me angry.

In my sleep, everyone is running away. I run too. I
start knocking on doors but no one opens any
door for me. I scream out my mother's name.
Then I see her head popping out of a doorway and
she says quietly, 'Come this way . . .' I run towards
her only to find myself facing a Talib, whose
weapon scares me. He makes me scream louder.
That's how I wake up. So, now I am also afraid of
sleeping. The ugly men have even stolen our sleep.

Masoma

*Earlier in the month, Masoma was in Pakistan for medical
treatment and was following the news from Aghanistan. She
realised Taliban takeover was inevitable and quickly travelled
back to Kabul to pick up her mother and travel overland to
Mashhad in Iran, where Masoma's sister lived. She anticipated the
Taliban would soon start imposing restrictions on women and*

knew this would make her and her mother especially vulnerable. They lived alone, Masoma caring for her mother, who has Alzheimer's. Masoma recalled scenes of the Taliban destroying gardens, 'like wild animals', the first time they took control of Afghanistan. She remembers it as a period of fear, a fear she expects to remain with her until her death.

These days bring back memories from the years
1997 and 1998. History is repeating itself at
speed.* I can feel the same fear, the same unending
and eerie silences, the same unpleasant news. At
that time, I was twenty-five and single. In the yard,
we had a water well. We told ourselves that if the
Taliban came, we would throw ourselves in the
well. Even in those days, writing was my bright
spot in life. With this thought, I get some peace.
Sometimes I think that Afghanistan is the end of
the world, where the sky is stuck to the earth.

એ

---

*The Taliban first ruled Afghanistan from 1996 to 2001. They gradually gained power and territory as a militia, before assuming control of the country. They were overthrown by an American-led invasion in 2001.

17 August 2021

Maryam

Maryam is twenty-five, living with her parents and siblings in Kabul. Unable to work or leave her home often, she reads every day. Her interest in politics followed from her interest in history and that in turn from her love of her homeland. She has never left Kabul.

This morning, I woke up to the sound of American military aeroplanes. Why is this happening? I've been thinking so hard about it. Why only surrender? Why not fight, rebel, resist? A government in the hands of the people is like playdough. Once we had it in our hands, why didn't we shape it the way we wanted? Or was this playdough in the hands of others, who have now shaped it in the way they wanted? Why is that sound still here: why are the planes not leaving? Now that they've made an agreement with the terrorists, what more do they want from this land? Maybe I should refer to historian Howard Zinn on the history of America, maybe I'll find answers there.

Maryam

The old man is right to ask why his military should fight for us when we do not fight for ourselves. But there is also this question: why did they come in the first place? Did they ask our permission to form us a government and choose us a president?

Maryam

Dear American airman, Dylan Elchin,* I
remember when you died in Ghazni. Dear
friend, do you know the country where you were
killed is now in the hands of your murderers?
What does it feel like to die at the age of twenty-
five? What kind of an experience is that? I am
the same age you were once, but I have a world
of hopes and dreams, for myself and for my
country. You must have had dreams too. I wish
we had a moment to meet and chat before you
were killed. I wish you might not have been
scared when you saw me, that you wouldn't have
pointed your gun at me and told me to *Stay
away, stay away*. I wish I might not have looked
at you as an invader. I wish we'd had a moment
to tell each other not to be afraid.

Maryam

Listen, Maryam. Calm down. It is good this way.
The old man and his military have left this
country. For this, I know you are happy. Don't
even think about who the murderers were. Think
only about what to do next.

Najla

Najla lives with her family in an apartment in Kabul.

We were all looking at each other, frightened.
The firing had stopped, but we were still scared.

---

*Dylan Elchin was a staff sergeant of the US Air Force killed by a roadside
bomb in Ghanzi Province in November 2018. He was 25 – Maryam's age today.

For two days we did not have electricity, but luckily today we had both water and electricity.

I opened the cupboards and took out some pasta to cook. My daughters were busy reading the news on their phones – if there was an update, they would read it aloud to me. My granddaughter Yasmin loves to eat pasta with yoghurt, the Afghan way. I slowed down the fire and called to my son to go out and get some yoghurt. He came back very quickly, saying all the shops were closed. I stood up with difficulty, one hand to my back and the other to the wall. The worry is affecting my body. I turned on the TV, but the national station only broadcasts the Quran now, and the Taliban congratulating each other on their victory. I took the pasta off the stove and cut up some tomatoes, onion and paprika to decorate our meal. Yasmin enjoyed her pasta; she looked at me, but she didn't ask why there was no yoghurt.

ॐ

18 August 2021

Marie

My parents worry most. They worry that I can't
work any more, that I can't walk out freely or dress
the way I used to. They worry this situation will
drive me crazy. I tell myself, calm down, be patient.
There will be light at the end of a long night.

At the end of the night, there is no light. Only
more people gone in the night, without telling
anyone where, without anyone hearing them
speak or feeling their pain. There is news of the
Taliban abducting journalists, interpreters,
artists and government employees from their
homes in the middle of the night.

I lie awake wondering how I can escape this
condemned land? I try to think of all the people
who can help me. I make a list for myself and plan
to send each of them a message in the morning. I
will ask if they can help to take me out of this hell.
What horrible words, what a humiliating situation.

Maryam

The Taliban have announced that they have
pardoned everyone. What was our crime that they
have pardoned us? Was being human our crime?
Was our crime that we considered Jews,
Christians and Hindus human too? Or was it that
we believed in elections and democracy, believed
them to be sacred?

Who are these people? Where have they come from?

Maryam

I'm sitting in my wheelchair. I always sit in a wheelchair, but today I think I live in a wheelchair. Previously I was unable to walk, but now I cannot even move. I struggled with my hands before; now it's worse. I was born disabled and now I've inhaled the air of dictatorship, I feel a lot more disabled.

ॐ

19 August 2021

Marie

At ten o'clock this morning, one of the girls
wrote on WhatsApp that the Taliban has now
started their house-to-house searches at night.
All day, I collected my records and books in a
bucket for my father to set fire to. We burned all
the books related to journalism and politics. We
watched each page burn to ash. With each page
that caught fire, a piece of my soul burned too. I
still haven't learned how to let go of the things I
love the most.

Maryam

From behind the window, I look at the moon.
My God, I haven't looked at the sky or the trees
for five days. Where have I been these five days? I
sit in my wheelchair, the world in chaos.

Autumn

The quince tree stands still and when the evacuation planes pass over it, its leaves shake gently, still absorbing the sunlight. The window is open. My silent room fills with the wind that has passed through the mountains to settle for a moment by a writer.

Maryam

2

My dear Kabul, give me your hand

20–28 August

Elahe, Tehran, Iran

Kabul-am, my Kabul, a broken city of hopes,
Watan-am, my land, a smoked land of dreams,
From now on, to witness your green valleys,
your running streams in your high mountains,
your wilderness full of red tulips,
your congregating doves above the blue domes,
to sit under your almond and apricot trees,
in awe of your Buddha statues,
I must go to sleep.

*It is now five days since the Taliban took control of the capital.
Born a refugee in Iran, Elahe has never lived in Afghanistan. Her
dreams of returning, even to see the country, have shattered with
the fall.*

Elahe

I am worried. I am worried about that girl who
finished her studies with a thousand hopes in her
heart. I am worried for all the girls. A friend told
me to pray that no more girls be born in
Afghanistan.

Since the day I was born and opened my eyes,
my name has been written on a piece of paper
that declares me an Afghan refugee. I was born
uninvited and without choice, a refugee who

could not be trusted. But I finished my education against those odds and wanted to be a part of building my country. The present situation has drained my pen and pierced my heart.

Zainab, Kabul

Zainab, twenty-five, lives in Kabul with her husband, whom she married just before the Taliban takeover. She works for a cultural institute as an administrator, reporter and photographer.

I have collected my documents, certificates, ID cards and all other paperwork that reveals my identity. When I look at these documents, I remember how hard I worked to obtain each one. I remember the days I went to university for half the day, spending the other half at a leadership training course for women. I skipped lunch to get where I wanted to be. I let my salary be deducted in exchange for leave to attend journalism workshops. I went on litigation courses despite my family's objections. I remember, once, I arrived home late at night, having obtained my anti-corruption certificate. My father was waiting for me in the alley with a stick. I was never sure why he brought it with him – whether it was to beat me or drive away street dogs. My hands shake to burn these pieces of paper that are my life.

Zainab

I heard two women in my neighbourhood talking to each other. One said: '*Khawarak,* sister, the Taliban won't do anything to you or me. We didn't have a seat in the government. We

didn't work with foreigners. We are still
illiterate. We still wear our *chadari*.* They won't
do anything bad to us. Why worry about anyone
else? If they stay inside their homes, Taliban
won't do anything to them either.'

I listened to their conversation and asked myself,
what is the difference between me and them?
After some thought, I put on a dress and wore
my red lipstick, as civil disobedience.

Marie, Kabul

For the past week, I've been trying so hard to
leave the country. I write emails to the
organisations I've worked with, asking them to
help me. I don't get any replies. I am so angry
and despairing. A lump rises in my throat:
fear and hatred, perhaps. It feels like a big ball
is moving between my heart and my mouth.
Every time it reaches my throat, I swallow it
down.

---

*Chadari is used most often in this book to mean the Taliban-approved
covering worn by women in Afghanistan, often blue. It covers a woman's
head and hair, with a mesh veil over her face, and then drapes loosely
over her entire body. Chadari come in different colours; brides wear white
chadari. Sometimes the Arabic word 'burqa' is used interchangeably
with chadari, and sometimes it carries an extra connotation of being an
imported form of dress, as the term is most associated with a similar
complete covering in black, worn in other parts of the Islamic world. An
abaya is a part of a burqa and a niqab is a variation with a slit at the eyes.
While the term 'hijab' is sometimes used to describe a simple headscarf,
covering a woman's head, hair and neck, it is also the general term for the
code of dress expected of women. This is now a code dictated (and
progressively altered) by the Taliban.

Our house is full of relatives, coming and going. Everyone is scared, terrified and helpless. Each one says to me, 'You're the educated one, you will find a way out for yourself. Find one for us too.' This request is so painful to me. It breaks my heart that I cannot add names to the evacuation lists. I can't admit this to my relatives because I know it will make them despair even more. I ask them to send me copies of their ID. I say that whenever there is a list, I will try to get them on it. I try my best to give them something to hope for. But I know this promise of evacuation by other countries is a mirage.

Marie is the middle child in her family, with two older brothers and two younger sisters. Her family call her the United Nations, always caught in the middle.

Fatima, Herat

Friday evening was dusty. The sky had turned red like blood. My mother and I went to my brother's grave. My mother kept saying, 'Oh God, why did you do this to us?' I poured some water on Hasan's grave. I am still in shock. I asked myself, now that he is martyred, who will be the breadwinner in our family? Now that my father is old and sick, who is going to take him to the doctor? At that moment, two men passed by the grave. They stopped and prayed alongside us. They saw my mother's anguish and said to her, 'Be patient, try to be easy on yourself.'

Nilofar, Mazar-e-Sharif

May his soul rest in peace.

Fatima

Thank you. May the souls of all the people who have passed rest in peace.

Zainab

May he rest in peace. He must have been young.

Parand, Kabul

May his soul rest in peace.

Naeema, Kabul

May he rest in peace.

Masoma, Kabul

May his soul rest in peace.

Mehrsa, Iowa, USA

May his soul rest in peace, I wish you patience.

Fatima

Thank you, all.

༄

Nora, Kabul

Salam all, does anyone know anything about the buses that transfer people with American and European visas from the Serena Hotel to the airport? Is there a phone number you can share?

Nilofar

Salam all, have you got an email?

Nilofar

They transfer only the people who have got visas.

Nilofar

I heard there was an armed clash at the airport. Does it mean the situation is getting more dangerous now?

Nora

Yes, they escort only people who have got their visas.

Nilofar

Lucky them.

Nilofar

Does it mean they are not allowing anyone to wait outside the gate of the airport?

Masoma

Oh God, I thought I was the only one who couldn't sleep due to worry and fear. It's past midnight and you are all awake too.

Nilofar

I've been worried since I heard about the clashes at the airport.

Nora

The people escorted to the airport are all classified in one category. Which category, I don't yet know.

Nilofar

If they are leaving from the Serena Hotel, they must be diplomats.

Farishta, Kabul

We have got our visas, but we can't get through.

Nilofar

Is it that hard?

Farishta

Unbelievably hard and crowded. You would think it's *roz-e-qayaamat*, Judgment Day.

Atifa, Herat

Insh'Allah, God willing, you will leave.

Farishta

It has been so difficult. Our hearts are cold.

Atifa

What is your destination?

Farishta

Canada.

Atifa

That's great.

Nilofar

What about these helicopters? Where are they flying people to? Are they helping to transfer people too?

No one knows what's happening. May there be
peace in Afghanistan. I hope you get through
safely, and safe travels.

Farishta

Thank you. I hope we all reach our destinations.

*At the moment this conversation is taking place, Samira is already
at the airport in Kabul, trying to navigate the crowds there and
board a flight. In the crush, her leg is injured and her phone lost —
the group does not hear from her again for two years.*

*Farishta's family was approved for evacuation to Canada
because they were considered at especial risk, on account of
their jobs and a history of being at odds with the Taliban. Her
brother was away studying medicine in Russia, while Farishta,
her mother and two of her sisters lived together in Kabul (her
father had died four years before). But two other sisters were
married and living elsewhere in Kabul with their husbands. This
posed a problem: the Canadian Embassy was only able to escort
the family to the airport from one house.*

*Nora's family did get on a bus, because of her husband's
protected status. But they spent two days on the bus just trying
to reach the airport, so they gave up and returned home. This
was just before the bomb attack* at the airport that killed 183
people and worsened an already terrible situation there. The
conversation above was also the last time the writers' group
heard from Nora for two years.*

✂

---

*Islamic State – Khorasan (IS-K) claimed responsibility for a suicide attack
at Kabul International Airport on 26 August 2021 that killed 170 Afghans
and 13 US soldiers.

Batool, Isfahan, Iran

Batool is a psychologist, a university teacher and an advocate of women's rights. In recent years, she has lived between Afghanistan and Iran, where she is finishing her PhD.

On 14 August, she was in a remote area of Afghanistan's Kandahar Province, doing research for her PhD, interviewing paedophile perpetrators. The owner of the guesthouse where she was staying told her the Taliban were coming and it would be wise for her to leave. Batool spoke to her husband in Kabul, who suggested she go directly to Iran as she wasn't far from the border and the children were already there, staying with Batool's mother in Isfahan. Batool escaped over the rooftops with just her phone and her passport. One of the men she'd interviewed for her research called and said he could see someone walking across the rooftops who looked like her. He said he would arrange for a car to pick her up and take her where she needed to go. When she descended to a quiet street, a car pulled up: 'Are you the doctor?'

Two days later, Batool arrived back with her children in Isfahan. From there, she followed the news of things collapsing in Afghanistan. She also faced difficulties extending her student visa in Iran: the authorities told her she would need to go back to Afghanistan to have it renewed. She was insulted at the visa office, and her son was insulted while trying to board a bus.

The man refused to give us tickets for the bus.
He said to my sixteen-year-old son, 'You are the
young generation of Afghanistan, you should
have stayed in your country to defend your land.
Take a weapon into your hands and protect
your land. Iran is tired of you, stay away from
Iran.'

I told him he was paid to issue tickets. That was his job, he didn't have the right to insult us and play political games with young people. I also told him he wouldn't know how it feels to have nothing in hand to protect one's homeland. The man pushed my hand away with hatred.

I saw exhaustion in the eyes of the other refugees standing in the line. Some were quivering as they stood waiting to get tickets. I felt insulted but I couldn't do anything except press my teeth against my lips. My daughters were afraid and held tightly on to me. In the end, two other Iranian men intervened and stopped the argument so I could buy my tickets. I said to myself, where shall I go and to whom shall I complain in this land with no head nor tail?

Batool
On the bus, I let all my tears fall. In the ticket office, I refused to let the tears of a refugee be seen. But now as the bus drove into the desert, I cried. I turned around, and all the Afghan passengers behind me on the bus were weeping too.

Nilofar
Safe journey, Batool jan.

Given the restriction on extending her Iranian visa and not fully registering the scale of change that had taken place in Afghanistan, Batool decided to take her children home to Kabul. When she announced her plan, at her parents' house in Isfahan, her mother thought she was joking. At the border, Batool saw people stream-ing out of Afghanistan but still didn't question her decision. Only once she arrived in Herat, found everything closed and men hanged in public, did she feel she had misjudged her return. She called her husband again. He was shocked to discover she'd returned to Afghanistan but set about making arrangements for Batool and the children to travel safely from Herat back to Kabul.

Masoma

It is so crowded everywhere. I wish it was a dream.
People are blocking the roads to the airport. Every
day, people die and are killed in this land. So
where are all these people coming from?

Parand

Parand, like Masoma, has bitter memories of the last period of Taliban rule in Afghanistan and the ways in which it delayed her independence in the world. She is indignant about being pushed back into that earlier state. The younger writers in the group look up to Batool, Naeema, Parand, Masoma and Najla as older and more worldly.

Our people have been in this vicious circle for
more than forty years. We are wanderers here.
We don't have a government. We don't have the
right to go to work or to dress our own way.
When we walk in the streets, we feel like
criminals awaiting their verdicts and sentencing.
They say Islam arrived to save women from
being buried alive as infants. If we had been
buried back then, they'd have eliminated us by
now and we wouldn't have to see this day.

Parand

Freedom is more vital for survival than food, water or air. And freedom is what we don't have.

ॐ

Zainab

Since she was a teenager, Zainab had been writing short stories, which she discussed with her brother, who is also a writer. She tried to write every day, even if she was tired after work. She set aside a little money from her salary each month to buy a new book.

I fill the pot with boiling water and add a little dishwashing liquid. I rip through my notebooks and journals page by page. With so much regret I immerse each page in the pot. My father reminded me that I couldn't hide the ashes of these notebooks if I burned them. He said if I soaked them in hot water instead, and washed them like clothes with good soap, there would be no traces of words left on their pages. He was right. The water in the pot has turned a lapis colour. Between my palms, I turn the soaked pages into blue balls and put them out to dry in the hot sun. Only then can I throw them out.

ॐ

Zainab

What's happening in Kabul tonight? No one can sleep. These attacks and explosions have no end.

We cannot do anything to protect our lives, and
neither can we protest all that's happening. We are
neither alive nor yet dead. I wish we had died
already so we did not have to die every moment we
live. If this land is not a place of living any more,
why can't they allow us to leave? I know they will
start killing each other again and let blood flow. I
am sorry for writing so harshly. I can no longer
shut down my feelings about what is happening.

Fakhta, Kabul

*Sent away from the university hostel in Kabul, Fakhta finally
sought refuge with distant relatives in Kabul, the ones she had
initially not wanted to trouble. From here she speaks on the
phone to her parents in Daikundi and her fiancé in hiding
elsewhere in Kabul.*

The Taliban went to my fiancé's home and
asked after his whereabouts. They told my
fiancé's mother that her son had collected
government weapons from his office and fled.
They told her she should ask him to return the
weapons.

We all know that when my fiancé came to Kabul
from Uruzgan,* he was not carrying even a pistol.
We know they were just making up an excuse to
arrest him. His family told the Taliban they didn't

---

*Uruzgan Province is a mountainous region in the south of Afghanistan.
From 2001, the province was subject to a struggle for control between
government forces and the Taliban. It was in the hands of Afghan government forces until 13 August 2021, when the provincial capital, Terenkot,
was captured by the Taliban.

know my fiancé's whereabouts. Without paying the slightest attention, the Talib said he should present himself in the district by a specific deadline.

We all know what would happen to him if he returned to Daikundi and surrendered to the Taliban. They know my fiancé very well. During the few months he served with the Afghan National Army in Uruzgan, he arrested many local Taliban during a fight that broke out.

We tried to find a taxi to send him outside Afghanistan but we couldn't find a driver we could trust. What's more, my fiancé doesn't have a passport, so our families decided to send him to Herat and from there to Iran with smugglers. We were all aware of the difficulties and hardships of going to Iran this way. But we didn't have any other choice. It is still better than his falling into the hands of the Taliban.

Fakhta

When my fiancé rang to say goodbye, I pretended to be the toughest person on the earth. I could feel the lump of pain in my throat, but I pretended to cough. In his sorrowful voice, he asked several times if I missed him. Each time, I said that now was not the time to be emotional and that we had to act with our heads. He even said that he would turn back if the separation was too hard for me. I knew if I showed any of my pain he would come back to Kabul and danger, so I stayed strong.

I ended the call, went to the kitchen, and cried out all my sadness there. We got engaged just a few months ago and had begun dreaming our best dreams of a shared life. He had taken a few days off to come to Kabul and we were planning to celebrate my birthday together. But since the Taliban came, I haven't been able to see him – not even to say goodbye. There is no corner for him anywhere in Afghanistan now the Taliban has taken over the whole country. If he stays, he will have to be in hiding for the rest of his life. So, he must go, and I must remain in Kabul with all my sadness.

೮

Maryam, Kabul

Maryam originally joined this writers' group because her sister saw an invitation to Afghan women writers to submit new stories for development and sent two of Maryam's along, aware Maryam would not have the confidence to do so herself. Everyone in Maryam's family knows about her writing except her father.

To be an artist in wartime is hardest. I shut the gate
to the world around me and I become nothing. If
wars keep happening in the world, then there must
be a solution for writers, painters, poets, musicians
and singers. For we must keep learning and working.

Maryam

Except for black tea, I cannot taste any other food
or drink. These days, no colour pleases me. No
tree is like before. These days my only comfort is
my family and the God whom we have blamed.

53

Today, after twelve days, I heard birds singing.
Instead of reading my book, I read the news.

Maryam

Panjshir,* I am your soldier. You are surrounded
by three thousand militia, can you survive? You
are my last hope. If you are also lost, what shall
I do? Panjshir, do not surrender. Do not give up.

Maryam

For the first time since the fall of Kabul, I went into
town. The whole city was sad and quiet. Men have
stopped shaving their beards; they stare blankly.
Women are not wearing burqas yet. They still move
freely, just like me and my sister. But covers have
been thrown over the mannequins in window
displays. I didn't see anyone laughing. I didn't even
see anybody smile, except a Talib in a yellow car.

Maryam

My dear Jewish neighbour, where are you these
days? Uncle Zebulan, do you still live in Kabul? I
just want to tell you that I am as restless as you
are. I feel as lonely as you do. Why do humans
have to feel this lonely? Uncle Zebulan, don't
worry, every human seems to have become
Jewish, wandering dismembered. These days, I
take my strength from you. May we all be safe.

---

*Panjshir Valley in north-eastern Afghanistan is the last enclave of the
country to resist Taliban takeover in 2021. There are reports of heavy fighting between Taliban forces and the National Resistance Front of
Afghanistan (NRF) throughout August and September. The Taliban had
never previously succeeded in taking control of Panjshir.

Maryam

I am awake. I listen to a Ghazal Sadat song that
goes 'You are here, with me, you are here, with me.'
I remember the days when I opened my laptop and
thought fearlessly about the characters in my story.

Maryam

I'm looking at the moon. Soon Lucy will look at
the same moon, and so will Negeen, Will and
Zubair.* But what distance there is between us
– how we see the moon and from where. Why is
the world not the same for all of us?

Kabul janam, my dear Kabul, you too are part
of the world. Even though they have made you
and me feel like we don't belong to this world
any more.

Maryam

What if the sorrow of the land was like the
sorrow of a woman? As a woman, if I speak,
every woman in the world seems to understand
my problems. But as a lover of my land, no one
seems to understand me, for this land is not
many people's land. My people have been
wandering for too long. Why can't another
country be my land? Why can't my land be
someone else's country? This war has made my
people refugees. My country isn't an urn that I

---

*Lucy, Negeen, Will and Zubair all worked for Untold Narratives, based in
the UK. Untold Narratives convened this writers' group and is in regular
contact with the writers.

can take with me anywhere I decide to go. It isn't
an earring or necklace that I can put on. I wish it
was a scarf, so I could wear it everywhere.

Kabul-am, Kabul janam, don't be afraid. You
can endure this too. You can be *azad*, free, as
you always wanted to be.

Maryam

My dear Kabul, give me your hand, put your
head on my shoulder and don't be afraid. Don't
think you are alone, we are here for you and
because of you. Dearest, you need to believe that
everything will be all right. Look at your moon.
The past few days, I haven't heard any
explosions in the city. Isn't that a good sign?
Take deep breaths and lean your tired body on
mine. *Mara bebakhsh, Kabul*, I am sorry, Kabul.

3
Visiting an uncle

Late August

Najla, Ghazni

Najla has lived almost her whole life in Kabul, but both of her parents came from the area around Ghazni.

Since I can't go to work these days, I decided to go on a short trip to the village where my mother was born. As a result of wars and revolutions, I have become a grandmother without ever having been there. In the old days, my job as a government worker meant it was too unsafe for me to try.

My son called the other day and told me on the phone that he was in Ghazni. As soon as I heard 'Ghazni', I panicked. Ghazni Province has witnessed the deadliest airstrikes in recent decades. The city of Sultan Mahmood Ghaznawi and Bayhaqi was turned into a graveyard of souls. I told my son off for risking his life to travel there. But he reassured me: 'Don't worry, the route is very calm and peaceful.' A day later he arrived in Kabul, and I could relax. I asked him about the journey. He told me, 'There are no checkpoints from Kabul to Ghazni as there used to be. No one asked me who I was or where I was going.' He told me he and his friends even explored the city in a car after midnight. I couldn't believe it. My son said that if I'd like finally to visit my mother's village, he would be happy to go with me.

My only maternal uncle still lives in the village with his family. I called to check on him a week ago – asking after my elderly relatives is a habit that brings me a little peace of mind. When I called this time, my uncle said he wasn't very well, so I thought it would be good to go and see him.

I opened my wallet and counted the money in it. I went to the market and purchased a few gifts for my uncle's grandchildren and some essentials for my journey. I started packing my bag, but I felt anxious. I wasn't sure I should leave my home – what if someone followed us and something terrible happened to us?

At 5 a.m. the next morning, I was still in two minds. I opened my wardrobe and took out my blue burqa. I bought it twenty-five years ago, the first time the Taliban took over Afghanistan and made wearing the burqa compulsory for women and girls. At the time, I had to spend a few months saving whatever little money could be spared from our daily expenses in order to buy the burqa. Over the years since that Taliban regime fell, every time I've cleared out my wardrobe, I've thought I should throw the burqa away. But I always wondered if I might need it again someday. Earlier this year, I finally decided to get rid of it. I took it outside and left it on the street for anyone to take. But no one touched it. So, in the end I brought it back in and returned it to the wardrobe. After twenty years, I now put it on to return to my mother's village with my son.

We took a Toyota Corolla taxi. The road was not crowded like it used to be. The taxi driver was a young man, maybe in his thirties. He told us that, before, there used to be a lot of tanks and military vehicles along this road, so if there had been any report of a security threat, every car on the route would be searched by the army. Sometimes it would take six or seven hours to reach Ghazni Province. But now the roads are empty, he said, we can reach it in three.

I observed a few lorries ahead of our car, full of families moving. Children were sitting on top of blankets, and I could see chickens tied up at their feet. These must have been families returning to their villages after being displaced by war. I felt suddenly happy that they could return to their homes and I daydreamed about them arriving at their destinations: rebuilding their lives, reclaiming their fields and getting back to an everyday life after a deadly war.[*] I disappeared

---

*The Taliban takeover in 2021 was preceded by years of fighting across the country, between Taliban and other militant forces against the Afghan national army and each other, driving many people to leave the violence in their provinces and seek temporary shelter in cities. What Najla sees here are families she imagines returning home after that fighting has ended. This movement of people driven by war is not confined to a particular

into my thoughts. My son sat in the front seat of
the car, beside the taxi driver. The Taliban don't
like women sitting in front with a male driver. I
know this from their last regime. On the way, I
saw damaged army vehicles and sandbags piled
up where there used to be checkpoints. There
was no sign of the national army. God knows if
the soldiers who used to be here are dead – their
lives lost for their country – or have surrendered
to the Taliban. I saw little girls walking along the
road in black dresses and white scarves, with
their blue schoolbags from the UN mission. Far
away from the city, this gave me hope.

We arrived in Ghazni, and my cousin rang to say
he would wait for me by the green Qala Mosque
in the village. Our driver was from Ghazni, so he
knew the place. My son pointed out the grave of
the poet Sana'i Ghaznawi, who was born in
1080, and I remembered his poem with the line,
'How would you get the pearls from the seabed
if like a child you are scared of the waves'. I
asked the driver to stop the car so I could see the
grave close-up, but he said there were Taliban
walking nearby. I saw a few young boys playing
near the grave. My son told me we could stop
at the grave on our return and pay our respects
to the poet's soul. There were still two and a
half hours to travel, around the mountains to
my uncle's house in our village.

---

period of Afghanistan's history. Najla herself remembers returning to
Kabul in 2001 after eight years in exile, to discover that the city she left of
500,000 people was now home to 6–7 million.

My mother's village is one that not a single
government has reached or served.
No government has built anything there in all
these years. The people who live in the village
farm their ancestral lands to produce all their
own food: from flour to milk and vegetables.
Two or three times a year, the young people of
the village travel to Ghazni to buy essentials like
soap, and fabric to make clothes.

As soon as we reached the village, I got out, so
no one in the village would see us enter in a car.
My cousins and their grandchildren came to the
front of the Qala to welcome us.

The silence of the village was occasionally
ruptured by the rumbling stomach of a cow or
the noise of children playing. Smoke from the
tandoor rose above us. It was fascinating: the
atmosphere was full of joy. After lunch, I quietly
asked my uncle if they would face any danger
because I had come to visit them from outside.
'No, up to now, there hasn't been any such
thing,' he replied. 'Before you, two or three other
guests came from a nearby village. We had food
and tea together and talked about the situation.'

We told him stories from Kabul, which he was
very keen to hear. My uncle said to me, 'I spent
forty-two years in and out of war and have never
seen such peace. I am glad the foreign invasion is
over, and the bombs have stopped.' His wife
said, 'I hope those times never come back. The
new government has brought peace.'

There was a photo on the wall with artificial flowers around it. My uncle's wife told me this was their son. He was in prison for five years, and soon after he was released, he died in a drone strike by the Americans. I said, 'Afghanistan is a graveyard of young men, women and children; of police, soldiers, engineers.'

We spent two days in the village, without TV, radio, the internet or the city's noise.

4

Restless days

28 August–16 September

In the immediate aftermath of the fall, the writers confront the detail of what it means to live in this new terrain: they struggle to get their documents from authorities increasingly hostile to women, they look for ways out of Afghanistan, they share news they've heard and notices about women's protests in Kabul. There is still firing: each time, they try to work out between them where and what it is. They are anxious for Panjshir Valley, the last area to resist Taliban takeover.

Nilofar, Kabul

Nilofar has travelled with some of her siblings and their families to Kabul, in hope of making it to the airport and out of the country. But while they were in Kabul the bomb attack on the airport (on 26 August 2021) took place and military flights ended. They must now make their way home to Mazar-e-Sharif, where they have lived since they returned from exile in Iran, when the Taliban fell twenty years earlier.

At the sound of flying aeroplanes, my sister and sister-in-law look hopelessly at the sky. I can hear their hearts say, *I wish we were on that flight*. It is so sad. They trusted me, but I made them wanderers. We are in a guesthouse. Only the children are running around happily. I've left my studies and I am so stressed here. The time has come for me to become a refugee, just like my grandparents and parents. I want to cry my eyes out, but then my family will see I am also in despair.

Marie, Kabul

At whichever door, whomever I talk to, I hear terrible words.

Canada is welcoming 20,000 more refugees. I tell myself it is a lie. These are rumours, or not for ordinary people like us.

Don't you have a foreign friend? This makes me angry.

You are educated. You'll end up leaving the country somehow. This makes me cry.

That person went to the airport, and now they're in Qatar. Why are you sitting here? Why didn't you go? If I were educated like you, I'd have been gone by now. I only look them in the eye.

Some people embrace me with sympathy. This drives me crazy!

Poor women, now they must not leave their houses.

What a pity, with all the education you had, now you must remain inside.

What is the point of working so hard, now nobody cares about you?

Your task is done here (said with an evil smile).

What's next? Just get married and settle down. He will provide for you.

It is good at least to see fewer girls in public places.

Nilofar

The Taliban are not allowing Hazaras* to enter
Kabul Airport. They have blockaded the
Pakistani border against Hazaras. There are
rumours that, in the aftermath of the American
retreat, the Taliban will massacre Hazaras
across the country. There is another rumour that
the interim government will be combined with a
return of Karzai and there will be no place for
Hazaras. I don't want to spread these rumours,
but my family panic and fear the situation and I
can't convince them they shouldn't.

Masoma, Kabul

Oh God, anything is possible under the Taliban.
For them, the Shia are infidels and the Taliban
think spilling infidels' blood is halal, permitted.
And so is stealing their women and wealth.

---

*Nilofar's family are from the Hazara ethnic group and made personally
anxious by concerns that the persecution of Hazaras will worsen under the
Taliban, because the Taliban carry a record of violence against Hazara
civilian communities from their first regime. Afghanistan's multiple ethno-
linguistic groups include Pashtuns, Hazaras, Uzbeks, Turkmen, Aimaqs,
Baluchis, Pashiae, Nuristani, Qizilbash, Gujur and Krygyz. At different
moments in the diary, the writers agree and disagree about the ethnic
tensions at work in different situations.

Maryam, Kabul

Salam dokhtara, did anyone hear the rockets?
Where do you think they hit? And who fired them?

Nilofar

Salam. A rocket hit a house near the airport.*
People say the Americans fired it. They also say
it was a safe house belonging to a member of the
DAESH† group, preparing to attack the airport.

Maryam

If that is the case, then it is a good thing. Even
though it is so scary, we still trust America. But
don't they have a defence system in place at the
airport?

Nilofar

So far, they say one child has been killed. Once
again, it seems like it is a political game and we
are only dice. I am not sure about any explosions
today. This was yesterday, I think.

Maryam

Yes, dear, that attack was yesterday.

---

*In retaliation for the airport attack, the US launched an airstrike in Kabul
on 29 August 2021 targeting a vehicle they said carried members of the
Islamic State group responsible (IS-K). The Pentagon later acknowledged
that target was mis-identified. Ten Afghan civilians were killed in the
attack, including seven children, all from one family.
†DAESH is an Arabic acronym for the Islamic State of Iraq and Syria (ISIS/
ISIL), that aims to establish a caliphate based on a strict interpretation of
Islam and is associated with violent attacks in different parts of the world.

Atifa, Herat

Dost-ha, friends, do you have any plans for leaving? There was another attack today.

Nilofar

I don't have any specific plans, dear. Has anyone from this group gone anywhere?

Atifa

I am not sure. It is so hard these days.

Nilofar

If I ever get the chance, I will go, for sure.

Atifa

You should.

Nilofar

I applied for refugee status, but they haven't got back to me with a reply. If I can, I might go to Tajikistan and see if I can apply through the UNHCR from there. If my application is accepted, I might get a yellow card and then leave for another country. Tajikistan is also a poor country, and not doing very well economically.

Atifa

It is very hard. It may take a long time for your application to be accepted.

Nilofar

I am not in a good place with my finances. I don't have the money to leave for any other

country. But I must go somewhere. I cannot stay
here. The Taliban will not allow me to work or
go to university.

Maryam

Dokhtara, if you are determined to leave, you
must not wait. All the international missions
have left Afghanistan. It seems the acceptance of
Afghan refugees is a deferred matter now. While
you wait, please take care of yourselves.

Nilofar

Yes, I've heard that we may not have a good
chance of getting refugee status anytime soon.

Maryam

It has always been so hard for me to leave the
country anyway. I tried for three years to leave
the country for medical purposes. Now it's
hopeless. We're all stateless.

Nilofar

Maryam jan, God forbid, why do you have a
wheelchair?

Maryam

Nilofar jan, this is a gift from God. One day I
will tell you about it.

Marie

*Many of the writers now need official documents, especially
those who hope to leave the country. For some of the writers,
born in times or places in which records were incomplete, this
means establishing their existence in state bureaucracy for the*

first time – just when it has become especially hostile towards women. Marie is one of the more hopeful of leaving, as she worked for an aid agency directly linked to the German government.

I've been going to the Ministry of Higher
Education for a few weeks now. The lane next to
the gate of the ministry is always crowded.
There are a few men there with dirty clothes on.
Their coloured shifts fall down to their knees,
and they wear red hats with mirrors
embroidered on to them. They just stand there
with long, matted hair, their military uniforms
on top of their clothes. They hold guns and look
right and left. When I see them, I am filled with
hatred and malice. But, at times, I feel pity for
them. They never got to experience goodness
and happiness in this world. Could there be just
one person among the thousands of them who
will realise they are wrong?

Today, a young boy about fifteen years old was
guarding the gate. As soon as I asked him about
my documents, he told me to come back in a
week. I asked him curiously if he had come from
another province. He said yes, with angry eyes. I
looked at his face. He had been standing in the
sun for too long.

Once again, I requested to go inside and talk
with the head of the office. The Talib grew
angry. As he did, he moved his hand on his gun
and said, forcefully, 'I am responsible for this
place. There are no documents here.' I retorted

that just last night his leader announced we could collect our documents. This Talib must never have come face to face with a woman who could insist and protest and demand answers of him. He became very angry. And that's what I wanted: to make him angry. I told him again that I wanted to see his boss. He got angrier. I told him that I wanted my documents so I could leave and find a job. I was frank, 'I don't wish to remain under your rule.' He said, 'Who are you to work? Where is your hijab?' Even though I was wearing a headscarf, you could see a little of my hair around my face. I replied, 'What is a hijab?' His eyes filled with venom. He furrowed his eyebrows till they were thicker than ever. 'Go before I kick you.' For a moment, I was scared. I imagined myself getting my answer with whips and weapons. My friend intervened and I returned home.

Freshta, Dushanbe, Tajikistan

Freshta's exile began two years previously. A journalist, she was forced to flee with her husband when the Taliban threatened the radio station where she worked.

My eyes are tired of waiting. I open my laptop and check for good news, but the wait is endless. For such a long time, I worked hard, studied. Then, in an instant, I became a refugee. I am in Tajikistan, waiting on asylum applications to more than ten countries. I haven't got any answer. Sometimes I think, if the situation gets better in Afghanistan, I will return to my country. But that hasn't happened either.

Everything has got worse. Where shall I go now? How long will I be without identity? When shall I forget myself?

No matter how much I try to comfort my baby in my womb, I cannot. I think I must be punishing her with my worries. I talk to my baby about the injustices of life. I am a refugee waiting for settled status, and I can move neither forwards nor backwards. I go to bed early but cannot sleep, I am very restless. I think about all that has happened to me and my country. I feel like I have an incurable disease.

∞

Sadaf, Kabul

Salam all, what is this firing for again? I am so scared.

> **Maryam**
>
> Seriously, I hear them too. What's happening?

Zainab, Kabul

I think there have been clashes between the Panjshir Resistance Front and the Taliban.

> **Naeema, Kabul**
>
> May God bring us peace. I also hear firing.

Zainab

The Resistance Front has come close to Kabul.

Maryam

I hope so, but who says this, Zainab jan?

Maryam

It seems very close. In our corridor, all the windowpanes are shattered.

Zainab

Then the firing must be very close to you, Maryam jan?

Maryam

Yes, too close. But I think it is calming down now.

Zainab

No, I don't think so. It is still happening.

Maryam

We are never informed about such things. But the fear and horror induced by this firing speak the loudest; the terrorists want to spread fear and horror.

Zainab

They've said for three days the situation is going to get worse. It is wartime, Maryam jan, everything happening around us is reality.

Maryam

Panjshir is still strong. The Taliban only entered the Parian Valley.

Zainab

Apparently, the firing is a celebration of their victory. They've announced their new Islamic Emirate government.* It's just their wild way of celebrating.

Maryam

I don't know any more. Everyone spreads different news. They said they wouldn't announce their emirate state until they captured Panjshir.

Zainab

Same here, I don't know anything. Everyone says different things. They're firing towards the sky as if they have finally captured Panjshir as well.

Zainab

I was so hopeful about the resistance forces in Panjshir. It seems our last hope is taken from us.

Parand, Kabul

My nephew is only two years old. He is so scared of gunfire. In the first two years of his life, he never heard gunfire. And now he is running from one room to the other out of fear. He keeps pointing outside, at the unknown.

---

*The Taliban title for the country is the Islamic Emirate of Afghanistan. From 2004 to 2021, the country was the Islamic Republic of Afghanistan. When the writers refer to 'the republic' it indicates that previous period.

My quince tree is in fruit. The laden tree feels so much cooler than the burning despair of Kabul city. Green leaves blow in each gust of wind and birds fly around the yard. Do they dare fly into town?

Maryam

Two days later

Zainab

Today's news is so upsetting:

The killing of Fahim Dashty,* a correspondent
and spokesman for the Panjshir Front;
Taliban infiltration into the capital of Panjshir;
The killing of a pregnant policewoman by the
Taliban, in front of her husband and children;
Burqa and black abaya forced on female
students.

My heart is full of sorrow and hopelessness.

> Naeema
>
> I hate the news, it is always bad news.

Rana, Kabul

I hope now the fighting is over.

> Naeema
>
> Dear Rana, the country is in the hands of
> *khonkhwaro*, the bloodthirsty.

---

*Fahim Dashty was the main spokesman of the NRF (National Resistance Front of Afghanistan) and a veteran journalist. He was killed during fighting between the NRF and the Taliban in Panjshir, almost twenty years to the day since he survived the suicide attack that killed the resistance fighter Ahmad Shah Masood on 9 September 2001. He was Ahmad Shah Masood's assistant at the time. A few days after Dashty was killed, Panjshir fell to the Taliban.

Rana

It was not in good hands before, either, there is no good leader in our destiny.

> **Maryam**
> ANNOUNCEMENT:
> Our promise: To Continue the Protests by Afghan Women Protesters
> Place: Kart-e-Char, in front of the Third Security District
> Time: Wednesday, 10 a.m.

Atifa

This is excellent.

> **Zainab**
> I am in, Maryam jan.

Maryam

All in good spirit, dokhtara.

> **Zainab**
> It is slowly becoming like a story of mine.

> **Zainab**
> Maryam jan, please send us a complete plan for the protest. Is everyone gathering at the location, or will there be a walk of some sort? Are both men and women allowed? What is the demand, what are we asking for? Is it about women's rights? Is it about supporting our previous military against Taliban rule? Or is it about asking the new government to stand tall against Pakistan?

Batool, Kabul

Dokhtara have gone towards the City Park.
They're gathering there right now.

৪১

A day later

Zainab

I became one of my stories' characters today. I
marched fiercely with thirty other young girls
and women, carrying slogans. The Taliban
looked at us with abhorrence. A few laughed at
us as they said things to one another. One of
them walked up and down, like a hungry wolf.
They would point their guns towards us if we
raised our voices. I kept telling myself to obey
what they commanded, or they would shoot us,
fearing no one.

We chanted our slogans of freedom to the
journalists who attended. The Taliban kept
suppressing our voices. They were increasing in
number and warned us about arrests. We did not
fear them.

In the end, the Taliban started attacking us
with their whips. I saw a ranger vehicle
stopping and three soldiers dismounting. We
started running in all directions. I heard their
whips flying in the sky. As I ran, I looked
behind me and saw them trying to catch us. We

kept running. I've been so afraid of attending
the demonstrations since yesterday. I have so
much fear and anxiety about facing the
Taliban, even though deep down I know that
whatever decision I make will be worth my life.
If I live, I will be so proud of myself for
standing against tyranny. With these
experiences, I feel I will be a better writer too.

*Zainab says before the protest they were afraid because demon-
strations had been expressly forbidden by a Taliban spokesman
and there were rumours they would be shot. On the day, she
went to the appointed place and saw only a few other women
there. They worried no one was coming. But the numbers of
protesters grew, and so did the numbers of Taliban. The Taliban
tried to suppress the protest – there was firing, beating and whip-
ping, even of journalists and cameramen. Some protesters and
journalists were arrested.*

Nilofar

I hope you are all right, Zainab jan. I am proud
of you.

Zainab

Thank you, I am all right, Nilofar jan.

Rana

Zainab jan, was Maryam with you too? I hope
everything goes back to normal.

Nilofar

I hope that too. As of now, all our hopes and
dreams are imprints on the water.

Zainab

No, Maryam could not attend due to some
personal difficulties.

&

The following week

Mehrsa, Iowa, USA

*Mehrsa left Afghanistan a week before the fall of Kabul, en
route to a Fulbright scholarship and master's degree in
America. Her dreams of returning to work in Afghanistan's
Ministry of Women's Affairs evaporated even before she left
home. She writes in from Cedar Falls, Iowa, where she feels
very alien.*

Everyone is texting me how lucky I was to leave
on time. I don't feel blessed or happy. The other
day, a lady called Julia came to my room and
invited me to sit with her in the hall. She held my
hands, closed her eyes and said, 'Dear Lord, I
pray for the safety of Mehrsa's family.' Her eyes
were closed, but tears crept out from under them.
I was surprised to find someone being so kind to
a stranger like me, and a non-Muslim too.

I feel like I have lost the image I had of living
here: one part of my life lies in darkness, while
in the other I struggle to try and bring my loved
ones to join me in safety. Even as I want to
advocate for them to everyone, I am tired. I want
to be quiet with my pain and not have to explain

the situation in Afghanistan to anyone. Still,
here people listen to me without noting I am
Hazara or a woman. This gives me comfort.

Nilofar

I want to go to Tajikistan. Does anyone know
how?

Freshta

I am in Tajikistan. I can help.

Nilofar

Thank you, Freshta jan. I will text you privately.

Atifa

Last night, I couldn't sleep, past midnight. I feel
like my sleep has migrated from this country
without me. It has taken my prayers and my
wishes with it. I thought perhaps the roof
blocked me from reaching God. So, in darkness,
I passed through the corridors and reached our
yard. I faced the sky and prayed.

*Atifa, a twenty-four-year old activist and aid worker, lives in the
city of Herat in western Afghanistan, where there had been
fighting the previous month – soldiers in Herat did not surrender
but fought the Taliban. It was in these battles that Fatima's
soldier brother was killed. Atifa's brother, also a soldier, fled the
country soon after the city was taken by the Taliban, to avoid
falling into their hands.*

Marie

Today I went to the bank. I looked around and
didn't see any changes in the infrastructure of

the city except for the long-haired men roaming in their latest cars. I still cannot think of a suitable name to describe such a reality. Apart from this, the saddest part of the city is the unfair and disquieting behaviour of men towards women now. They wear a look of victory and dominance. I arrived at the bank and a man angrily asked me to step aside, without even looking at me. He reasoned that the Taliban might find my presence provocative – as if it were my fault. I might cause a disruption.

This is not an attitude you find only at the bank. In restaurants, buses and everywhere, this is what's happening. Everywhere women go, they are insulted. There is no one to break this pattern, as everyone fears each other.

Among the hardest things Marie has had to do this month is to close the counselling service she founded with a friend. Marie spent almost all the hours not filled by her full-time job working for this service, called the Meaning of Life. It offered child counselling, marriage counselling and educational counselling. After the bombing of Sayed-ul-Shuhada* school, the Meaning of Life offered voluntary support to people who had been affected, visiting them at home. But staffed entirely by women, it is no longer able to continue its work. Batool also worked as a counsellor in this service.

---

*On 8 May 2021, a car bomb was detonated outside the Sayed-ul-Shuhada High School in Dasht-e-Barchi. When students rushed out in a panic, two more bombs exploded. More than 85 schoolgirls were killed in the attack and more than 150 injured.

Fakhta, Kabul

It is almost two weeks now since my fiancé left for
Herat. Although I couldn't see him in Kabul, his
presence gave me a lot of strength. Since he left, I
feel like I am on a different planet. He left his SIM
cards in Kabul before leaving for Herat. I can
rarely talk to him on the phone now and I know
he's trying to cross the border into Iran.

I've also lost hope of the university reopening. I
asked my father if he could help me get back to
Daikundi and he managed to find a relative of
ours who will drive me.

Maryam

Kabul-am, I don't have the energy these days to
write or even think. I am busy with thoughts of
war. I have a headache. I have a fever. I feel like a
river of blood has left a moving wave in my
brain. My dear city, give me your hands and
believe that in war and peace, I will always
remain your artist daughter.

Kabul-jan, I won't allow your pain to be
forgotten. My dearest, I promise you, I won't
allow you to go artless. I will decorate you
myself, with my art. Let them see you fall to
pieces. You just be patient and remain proud.
On one of your bitterest days, I managed to
publish a story. I dedicate this story to you. I
hope you will accept this token of my promise to
you. I am Maryam, your ever worrisome friend.

So present until now, Maryam disappears from the collective conversation for months. She says that as she read the diary in the autumn, she realised that everyone else was interacting with the world outside whereas she only knew the inside of her own home. If you want to picture her, she says, see her sitting in her wheelchair with her books, her notebooks and laptop, in her room above the quince tree.

ॐ

Batool

It is 1 a.m. I hear a voice message pop up on my WhatsApp. It is in one of the groups that participated in the latest protest. I play it. The voice is trembling. She says, 'Dokhtara, be aware, be careful, the Taliban are going from home to home, searching for girls who were present at the protest . . .'

Slowly all the girls start to come online, all those brave souls trembling now. There is an exchange about what to do, then, 'Dokhtara, please stop using the internet from now on . . . be careful.' The group chat is now silent. I feel as if, drop by drop, I am turning into water. One by one, I pray for each protesting girl, in my dark room.

Batool is currently at home in Kabul, where she has been involved with the women's protests since her return to Afghanistan three weeks ago. The protests began from the moment women knew they were staring oppression in the face, she says. Within the group they debated how to go about it – should they comply with the Taliban dress code or should they go as themselves? They decided to remain as they were. Each time, they would find a public place to settle, inviting journalists to come there and hear their demands. In the beginning, Batool says, they only knew how to enter a protest, not how to leave one. Gradually, they became experts in how to run away.

5

A false return

Mid-September

Fakhta, Daikundi

*Fakhta was six months old when her family first fled the Taliban.
They went first to Pakistan, then lived as refugees in Mashhad
Province in Iran, close to the border with Afghanistan. The family
returned to Afghanistan when Fakhta was four. She loves her
home in Daikundi – mountainous and dry, famous for its almonds.*

As the road brought me closer to Daikundi, I felt
more and more distant from my studies and my
fiancé. I kept thinking, had I stayed in Kabul,
maybe I would have a better chance of seeing
him again – it would be impossible for him ever
to come to Daikundi. But then I remembered my
parents were waiting to receive me and that
brought a smile to my face.

I arrived home around breakfast time. My father
was at his clinic. He is a doctor and goes to work
very early. I had breakfast with my mother, and
she joked that now my father was thinking of
taking us all to Kabul. I asked what his reason
was, but she didn't know. I didn't think any
more about it. I went to take a nap.

My mother woke me up for lunch. When I
walked into the hall, I saw my father sitting

down to eat. He never usually comes home for lunch, so I was surprised. I said Salam, and we all had lunch together. My father looked stressed and somehow depressed. I gestured to my mother to ask if she knew why? She shook her head. I couldn't bear the look on my father's face, so I asked him what was wrong. He was silent at first. Then he turned to face us and told us what had happened.

My father had got a phone call the previous day from an unknown number. The man at the other end of the call spoke Pashto. My father has enough Pashto to reply, so he returned the man's Salam and then asked what he was calling for. The voice said, '*Dokhtar-e tu ra mekhaham*, I want your daughter,' and started to laugh. My father hung up and blocked the number.

My father is a doctor, and a mild man. He has always been very nice to everyone. He believed that the call must have been from one of the people looking for my fiancé, most probably the same Talib who went to visit my fiancé's mother. My father believed that, since they hadn't been able to reach my fiancé, they were now trying this manipulation to get him to return to Daikundi for my sake.

The thought brought so much anxiety and fear among us. My father was more stressed than anyone. He kept saying that if they had a problem with him, he wouldn't mind but he was terrified they were bringing me into it. I saw he had lost his peace of mind and felt I had now become a headache to my parents.

To have more space to think, my father switched off his phone. Yet our days were still anxious. My parents could not sleep at night: my mother recited the Quran and prayed; my father walked up and down the yard. And I was too scared to close my eyes.

My father managed to speak to my fiancé and asked him to stay in Herat and not to go to Iran until we knew what to do next. After five days, my father switched his phone back on. Within three hours, the person called again and repeated the same words. My father got very restless and left the house. We waited for him in the yard. After forty minutes, he returned. He faced us again. 'Pack your things, we are to make a journey tonight.'

He then called my fiancé with his new plan: 'We've booked a car to take us secretly to Kabul tonight and from there to Herat. I am bringing Fakhta with us. I'll give her hand into yours, so wherever you go, you go together.'

During the last Taliban regime, some twenty-two years ago, I was six months old when my parents migrated to Iran due to Taliban oppression. My father knew only too well what it meant to be smuggled across a border. He acknowledged that life would be difficult for us but said, 'Despite this journey's hardships, I prefer my daughter to be far from this land of wrath.'

We did as my father chose. In the middle of the night, all three of us – my parents and I – walked towards our ride to Kabul. I remember we left Daikundi at exactly two in the morning. I wished I could say goodbye to my friends and to our village for the last time, but we left without telling anyone we were going.

Towards an unknown fate, we all kept moving.

I hear leaves. The quinces are in the jam pot.

Maryam

6

We won't vanish

A month from the Taliban taking charge, some of the writers return to work, and schools reopen. This is when the announcement comes that everyone has been dreading.*

Marie, Kabul

I don't know exactly how long it has been since
the arrival of the Taliban, but the city still smells
of fear.

People have returned to the market. But street
vendors have receded from the frightened face of
the city.

Seeing other humans in the city makes me feel
calmer. But the saddest scene is to see a city
without women. In the absence of women,
Kabul has lost its colour.

The city is filled with men in long dark clothes.
Now, it is hard to tell the difference between the
Taliban and ordinary men who have started to

---

*In relation to women's ability to work and schools reopening to both boys
and girls, the picture is not clear or consistent across the country. In both
cases, Taliban statements are contradictory and sometimes other constraints
– such as those on women's dress and travel – have a prohibitive effect. But
what is clear is that secondary schools do not reopen for girls.

dress like them. With so much anger I want to
say, *You cowardly men, goat-hearted men,*
treacherous, self-serving men.

Nilofar, Kabul

The Taliban have stopped girls from going to
school.

Girls are like glowing lights in the middle of a
dark night. They have turned off those lights.
I am sure they will also ban women from
going to public universities. Each day,
Afghanistan is going back into a bleaker era.
I'm scared of the day Afghanistan falls into
complete darkness.

Rana, Kabul

Today's announcement broke my heart.

Rana is a teacher. She teaches Pashto literature in secondary
school. She has just returned to teaching after being sent home
from school, as Sadaf was, on 15 August, in the middle of setting
her students an exam.

Fatima, Herat

Since the day of the fall, I have been very
worried. But I didn't lose all hope. For they said
the Taliban would allow women to be educated.
I waited weeks for the university gate to open so I
could go back to my studies and find a job to
support my elderly parents. But now I have lost
all hope. The Taliban said that boys can go back
to school, and men can go back to work. But
girls can only return to school up to Year 6. I am

so helpless and there is no way of fleeing this country either.

A soldier in the national army, Fatima's brother was killed in combat less than a month ago, in the battles to ward off Taliban capture of their hometown. Amid their grief, the family is also living in fear because of their connections to the military: Fatima's mother worked as a police officer on one military base and her father worked in the kitchen of another. Fatima is anxious to complete her degree in English Language and Literature.

Naeema, Kabul

Naeema is a teacher in Kabul, teaching girls in the morning and boys in the afternoon.

Yesterday I spent the whole day in great difficulty. I listened to news and analysis all day. I had a headache, and I was not feeling well. Today, I got up early in the morning and went to school. The head teacher had said, 'When you do not have lessons, do not come to school.' I did not have a lesson, but I went anyway just to change my mood.

I got in the car, but the driver would not allow me to sit in the front seat. 'If you want to sit here,' he said, 'you have to pay for another person.' I asked him, 'Why would I pay double?' Someone else told the driver to hurry up. 'We will be late. If she wants to pay, she can stay. Otherwise, she needs to get out. We used to listen to these women – that time is gone now.'

One of my friends told me that her husband has behaved differently since the Taliban came. She said he doesn't listen to her now, though they used to discuss many matters before. She said, 'He told me I needed to shut up and not get involved in his matters. Take care of the kitchen and the cooking.' She said her husband was speaking to his friend on the phone, and they congratulated each other that women's rights were gone. When all the signs of authority act against you, people will also show their hang-ups.

Najla, Kabul

One day, when I looked at my phone and turned on the internet, I saw a text from our manager. It said that the office would reopen on Sunday.

'You need to be at the office at 8 a.m. The ladies need to sit at the back of the office van, and their workspace is separate now. I hope you will all accept these changes.'

I'm back at the office now, a month since I was last in. Our whole team used to work in one open-plan office. Now the women are in a separate room. The printer is in our room, so every half hour or so on the first day, a male colleague would come in to pick up printouts. One of them knocked on the door and checked no one was standing near the printer as he entered. He was so nervous, he tripped. I don't know what he was thinking.

Marie

Before the fall of Kabul, there were rumours the
Taliban were coming back, so the price of burqas
went up. One burqa cost between two and four
thousand, and it was considered a valuable object
to carry in the shops. Everyone had started feeling
helpless with the news of many provinces being
captured by the Taliban. There was a recurring
conversation about how the Taliban had no more
than a few thousand members: how would it be
possible for them to take hold of the entire
country? Yet everyone seemed silently to have
resigned themselves to the victory of the Taliban.

But the good news is that women still didn't buy
the burqas and appeared in public in their usual
clothes. Not only that, but they went to protests,
raising their voices, in the same clothes. I deeply
appreciate these women.

Everyone has their own path to take, and we are
different from each other. But I am happy that
we are not the women of 1996 any more. Each
of us in some way takes a step forward so that
the future is ours.

Zainab, Kabul

It is as impossible to change me and other
educated women as it is to change the Taliban.
The Taliban do not accept progress, and we do
not accept regression. If we try to put these two
in an equation, there is the Taliban government
and then there is us, my friends.

Batool, Kabul

The way of fighting has changed. Early this morning, we came to the streets in support of the teachers' protest. We faced the Taliban once again. They confiscated the cell phones of our comrades, Hameda and Razia. We fought back and changed the face of our fight. We walked to the Kabul Chehel Sotun Garden and waited there. We called other women and united in one place. We also called foreign and local media channels and invited them to our fight. From the outside, it looked as if we had gathered for a picnic. We chanted our slogans about women's rights and demands. After the reporters left, the Taliban appeared at the gate of the garden. I don't know who had reported us, but they started interrogating us. We had a few Pashto-speaking women among us, so they spoke with the Taliban, and it all ended with a little more understanding.

Being among these brave women gave me so much confidence, even though the situation felt very frightening. It was my first time standing so close to the Taliban and facing up to them.

We are planning our next gathering. We will have tougher days ahead of us, but I also have hope. Long live the brave women of Afghanistan.

The women's protests took place not only in Kabul but also in other cities of Afghanistan. Among the main demands they made were that girls should continue to go to school, that universities remain open for young women and that women should be able to work. The Taliban responded by flogging, abducting and imprisoning women. There was also the fear of dishonour, Batool reminds us, if the Taliban abused women in custody. When one young girl she knew returned home after being interrogated by the Taliban, her own family wouldn't open the door to her. Fear spread like a rash, Batool says. Known activists were compelled to flee the country.

ॐ

Naeema

The Taliban can never keep girls from education.
Today's girls are not the girls of twenty years ago.
If they try to do this, they will not remain in power
for longer than two years. An awakened society
cannot be erased, because it will keep fighting.

Naeema loves her job as a teacher. She says she wasn't particularly interested in children when she began working but the job changed that. She says, 'The generation I taught – I taught to do the things I wasn't able to do when I was their age.' She also runs a foundation that publishes books for children.

Najla

Jamila and Tahmina are my youngest daughters.
Jamila is eighteen years old, and Tahmina is
sixteen. Both study at a private school in Kabul.
They are in Year 12* and only have a term left

---

*School in Afghanistan runs from Year 1 to Year 12. A student in Year 1 would typically be 7 years old but education for children in Afghanistan

before they are due to finish school. Since 15 August, when the Islamic Republic of Afghanistan collapsed, they've not been able to go to school. Yesterday the Taliban announced that secondary schools for boys would reopen and boys could go to school from Years 7 to 12. This did not apply to girls. When my girls heard the news, they were very angry and despairing.

I found them praying when I brought them tea, and both later came and sat next to me during our nightly prayers. They looked at each other and laughed. Then both looked at me. I smiled and asked what was happening: 'Have the two of you made a plan?' Tahmina looked at Jamila and said, 'You tell Mori.' They started to argue over who would tell me. I lost my patience and asked them just to say what they wanted to say.

Jamila said, 'Mori, please allow us to go to our school tomorrow.'

I was surprised they were asking me this.

'How will you defend yourself when the Taliban punish you?'

---

has been continually disrupted due to conflict and it is not unusual for classes to contain students of different ages. For girls, this is particularly true: even in this writers' group some writers went to secondary school in their twenties, their education having been disrupted by conflict, earlier Taliban decrees or family reluctance to send girls to school. It is a broad group of both girls and women who are restricted again by the closure of secondary schools for girls.

Tahmina said very cautiously, 'Don't worry. We only want to see our teachers. All our classmates in the WhatsApp group are agreed.'

I told them angrily that I could not take such a massive responsibility. Both sat next to me, hugged me and started to beg.

In the morning, they both wore their headscarves and facemasks. When I looked at them, I saw ordinary schoolgirls, gorgeous in their dark green tops with checked black and green skirts and black scarves. When they said goodbye to me, I knew they were laughing under their masks. They left saying, 'Don't worry, we will come back in the afternoon.' I wasn't too anxious as their father was going to drop them at school.

At 11 a.m. I got a call from Jamila saying, 'We want to go to a restaurant to have lunch. Then we will come home.' I was livid. 'If the Taliban see you, what you will do?' I cut off the call. She called me back and said her teacher and Miss Parisa were also going with them, so I said, 'OK, you can go, but at 1 p.m. your father will pick you up.'

They came home at 1.30 p.m., both looking happy and eager to tell me what had happened.

They said, 'Thank you, Mori, for allowing us to go. We met our teachers and classmates, all of them wearing black headscarves. We had a lovely day. After lunch we had chocolate cake.'

Nilofa Sharif

Now ba e in Mazar-e-Sharif, Nilofar still works when she is able e travels with a project supporting disabled people but e her brother with her. If they encounter Taliban check n the way, she may be expected, as a woman, to have a mahra le chaperone from her own family.

Along the whole ro m Khashinda back to Mazar, I cried. I crie tly, so that my brother and the other men in t would not hear me. The village people are c with the situation. They think it is now the fighting has stopped. They say they have to be afraid of checkpoints, explos r landmines. It is true that it is better in that e.

No explosions, no landmines, no s de bombings. But there is also no laugh no happy music, and no loud voices tellin tories. We used to be afraid of travelling this rote, but once we crossed the local Taliban checkpoints, we would feel alive. Now I just cannot stop my tears. When we arrived in Aqerak Bazar, the place was filled with Taliban. For fear of the Taliban, I couldn't even take a picture of the river when crossing the bridge. I wished I could throw a handful of water over my head and face.

Previously when I used to cry, I felt relieved. Now after crying I feel more depressed. As one of my friends says: 'These days, we are alive, but we don't live any more.'

Zainab

The Taliban government officials have only
one general instruction to carry out: violence.
They approach the protesters' demands with
their whips and bullets. When they encounter
a traffic accident, they settle disagreement by
beating both parties. To regulate congested
traffic roundabouts, they give electric shocks
to those on bikes. They think this way, the
traffic will move faster. They implement every
Sharia law by pointing their guns at people's
heads.

Nothing good can be expected from such people.

Half of the people in this country were killed
in explosions and suicide attacks by ISIS; the
other half are mourning their loved ones.
Some are fleeing the country while others are
left starving and waiting for death from
hunger and poverty. This is the price we pay
for being Afghan and being born in a
geography of war.

Rana

You have said it so beautifully, Zainab jan.

*Rana stopped writing much in the diary, not feeling safe enough
to share her thoughts and feelings in the new climate of
Afghanistan. But she kept reading, keen to hear what others were
experiencing in different places and wishing to stay connected to
a group of which she felt very much a part.*

Nilofar

Facebook is filled with images of household goods. You can find them in Herat, Kabul and Mazar. From the pictures, you can see that these objects haven't been used before. It is so sad to think, each time, that a woman in Afghanistan must have bought these goods for her home with hope, and now she marks a price for selling that hope.

Nilofar

A few days ago, I met one of my former students in town, selling grapes on a cart. I felt so terrible. His father was a soldier. If the government had not collapsed and his father hadn't lost his job, he might have been in his class, learning. A teacher's dream is always to see her students have a brighter future as a doctor, an engineer, or an artist. But I see with my own eyes and in theirs that their future has been annihilated. When I said hello to Reza, he said he wanted to go to Iran with smugglers. He said by going to Iran, he could have a more promising future. I know for certain that in Iran he will be a labourer and will not have a bright future.

Nilofar

These days, even my pen feels heavy on my fingers. I cannot hold it. Perhaps I am unstable, I am weak. Truth be told, I am hopeless and helpless. This disables a person. My heart wishes to write. I want to write. I wish to write a

novel about my country and what it has gone
through in the past two months. But I am scared
I won't be able to write it. I've lost my
motivation. I need some encouragement to pick
up my pen and write down all the things we have
witnessed, the things we've lost, and how our
lives have dissolved into uncertainty.

Marie

We are the moving dead bodies.

In the morning, we pour ourselves tea.
We prepare breakfast,
We wash the dishes.
We clean and dust every place,
We go shopping in the city.

We say hello to one another,
We smile at one another,
We shake hands.

At night, we carry our bodies back to bed with
    us.
We are the moving dead of this century.

Oh, the wanderers of the twenty-first century,
Whereabouts on this earth were our souls
    buried?
When did the pieces of our bodies fall apart?
On which bridge did we lose our feet,
That we never get anywhere in peace?

7

Insh'Allah you will arrive safely

Late October

I feel like a turtle whose entire load sits on its back. When you become a traveller, you will understand that you cannot take everything with you. Carrying a pair of socks adds weight to your load. When you become a traveller, you will learn how to detach your heart from those you love the most, you know the best. You will feel sad to leave the house you grew up in and the alleys you played in. You will feel lost and need to become more patient. Now I am a traveller, I am with the turtles and the birds.

Zainab

☙

Najla, Kabul

I went to a travel agency in Wazir Akbar Khan area in Kabul. I asked after a visa to Pakistan and they told me that the visa is sold with the travel ticket. I wondered how much that would come to and they said 2,500 US dollars per person. My God, it is beyond reason. We cannot go, we don't have that much money: we are a large family. We can't even take the land route – I have young girls, and it is very dangerous. I don't know what to do.

Freshta, Dushanbe, Tajikistan

In Tajikistan, Freshta's husband can only find jobs on dangerous construction sites and she can't find any work at all. She tries to read but she can't afford glasses. She is twenty-four, pregnant with her first child.

I spend the whole day at home. From my window, I can see a house that always has a window open. Sometimes a person sits there watching the street.

I love the season of autumn. I want to step on the leaves, listen to music and speak to someone who never tells me anything but listens to me. I like the outdoors, but I don't want to speak to people. I can't stand it when other women talk about make-up, shopping or beauty salons. I cannot find someone like me. So, I am with myself most of the time. Sometimes I am so much with myself that I forget to go out and see nature.

I make some tea for myself and have it with dried fruit. I either read or listen to audiobooks because I have no hard-copy books. And my eyesight is so weak nowadays that I can't even read PDF books. Sometimes I think a lot and realise that I haven't moved from my spot for hours. I think about the future, to forget about the present. I used to listen to music, but nowadays I feel so lonely that I can't find a song I like.

Yesterday I sat alone and unable to understand why I was upset or what I wanted. Suddenly I felt movements in my stomach, and I remembered I was not alone. I have my baby with me. She is beautiful, like an angel. She is strong and walks with me; she knows how to listen to a mother who lives far away from her homeland as a refugee.

Fakhta, Herat

When Fakhta describes herself as engaged, she means that she and her fiancé have performed the religious nikah *ceremony that consecrates their marriage, a few months previously, in the presence of close family. They were due to have a wedding at a later date, which would have marked the beginning of their life together. In the present circumstances they forgo this second ceremony. Fakhta's parents travel with her to Herat, pretending they need to take her to a doctor there, so they can take her to be with her husband.*

Never have I been interested in luxuries, nor cared much about customs or traditions. But like any other girl, I imagined wearing a white dress on my wedding day and starting my new life surrounded by friends and family and dancing.

My husband had even bigger dreams. He wanted us to have a house and car before marriage. But with the arrival of the Taliban, all those dreams and aspirations were demolished. Instead of a white dress, I began my married life in the same dusty dress in which I travelled from Kabul to Herat. My husband's army salary has been suspended, so we used the money my father gave

us as a wedding gift, to rent a small house in the
back alleys of Herat. We have furnished it with
second-hand goods collected by my husband's
relatives and in it we've started our life together.

Najla

Today I could not sit at home, so I went to a
different travel agency and asked about a visa
and ticket to Pakistan. The agency staff replied
that all flights are cancelled until further notice.
I felt very anxious. All the borders are closed. I
asked the airline agent there about visas to Iran,
and he told me, 'You get those from shops in
front of the embassy.' I went there and saw there
were long queues.

Masoma, Stockholm, Sweden

*This is the first anyone has heard from Masoma since August.
She travelled to Iran to hand her ailing mother into the care of
another sister who lives there and set off alone on a dangerous
journey westwards. She travelled from Iran to Turkey overland
and from there by sea to Greece, all arranged by human smugglers.
Masoma then made her way by boat to Italy and north through
continental Europe by train. Even today, she struggles to find
words to describe what a terrible journey it was. She told herself
that, wherever she arrived, she would stay there until she died.*

Salam, dear writers, I hope wherever you are,
you are doing well. After a long time, I finally
came to Sweden. I hope one day you too find
yourself in a safer country. I wish you all the
best.

Nilofar, Mazar-e-Sharif

Thanks be to God that you've reached safety.

Freshta

So glad you've arrived safely.

Najla

Salam, Masoma jan. Thanks for sharing this happy news. I hope you arrived safely and wish you all the best. Ameen.

Masoma

Thank you, dear friends. May you be safe and well, wherever you are.

Naeema, Kabul

May you be safe, Masoma jan. I hope one day no human being will have to leave their homeland in order to be safe.

Rana, Kabul

Ameen. Salam, dear Masoma, I am so glad you arrived safely and wish you a calmer and better life there.

Masoma

Thank you all. I wish for the day we all have peace and prosperity.

Masoma

My heart wishes for happiness. Like people with a country that belongs to them, I want a free country, so I can walk free, so I can yell from the top of its mountains. I would shout out that I love you.

I want a free and peaceful country, without the cruelty of the Taliban. I want a land where innocent people are not killed at the hands of fanatics. I want a land full of kind, thoughtful, human beings.

Batool, Kabul

Salam, my dear Masoma, I miss you here. I am still in Kabul. I hope you won't forget us, my dear.

Masoma

Salam, my dear Batool, I also miss you and your little kids. I had no option but to leave. I hope you will also leave sooner rather than later to a safer country. Until then please take care of yourself.

ॐ

Nilofar

They say the roads are safe now. Of course, it should be so because the Taliban themselves control every checkpoint. But when you travel in a bus, there are no chats and conversations among travellers, people don't laugh any more. No one carries sunflower seeds as snacks. No one dares to listen to music, or sing songs, especially if there is a mullah travelling on the bus. Everyone prefers silence. This silence is boring.

If anyone tries to speak, it is considered a
criticism of the Taliban. So, everyone stays
quiet. No one has the right to criticise the
Taliban government. I remember reading about
Stalin's era in our Russian history class: it was
described as a period of total terror and horror.
That is exactly our situation right now. Sadly,
this is how I came to define freedom for myself.
In its absence, I think I know what freedom
means.

Fakhta, Herat

Since I found a book to keep myself busy, my
mental situation is better. My husband also
brought me pens and paper. From time to time, I
write down all my worries and pain.

Being in Herat is very hard for my husband. I
spend time reading my book, but my husband
can't do much. He can't walk about freely
because he was in the army and must not be
recognised. Before the fall, he was a keen
sportsperson. He used to go to the gym and
never stopped training. At least now he has
found a football pitch where he spends a few
hours playing football, each week. That is
helping his spirits.

Our mental condition is getting better, but we
still have to contend with poverty and having no
jobs. My husband has tried to find a job, I've
tried to get a job in a school, but each time we
were rejected. We had to pay the rent and bills at
the beginning of the month. Once we had

cleared all that, we only had money for two weeks' worth of food.

The only solution to our misery in Herat is to go to Iran illegally. We know living in Iran is not going to be easy either, but this is our last option. Kabul and Daikundi are out of the question. To stay in Herat would be to remain homeless and miserable. So, we have decided to go to Iran illegally. We've packed up our stuff and emptied the house before the next month's rent is due. At dusk we leave for Nimroz,* where a smuggler is waiting to take us to Iran.

Marie, Kabul

Marie is able to leave Afghanistan on a German government scheme because she worked for a German organisation. She will travel with many former colleagues and their families; in her case she is going alone.

I am very sad. A few days ago, I was contacted and told to bring all my documents to prepare for travel. Next week I will probably fly and leave my country forever. I try to stay happy, but I cannot. Something is lying very heavy on my chest. I feel no emotion, as if I don't care to go. I

---

*Nimroz Province is in the south-western corner of Afghanistan. It borders both Iran and Pakistan. In recent years, Iran has built a 5-metre-thick concrete wall that runs more than half the length of its border with Afghanistan. To get around this wall, those looking to reach Iran are often smuggled across two borders: first from Afghanistan to Pakistan and then over Pakistan's border with Iran.

will escape, but my family, parents, siblings and friends will have to live and breathe here under the rule of these horrible bearded men.

I worry how my mother will bear the longing. All her children are leaving her, one by one, when she needs them the most. What kind of children are we, really? When I think about my father, my heart breaks. How can I tell him that I am going away and I will not come back?

I am scared that when I meet my parents again, their eyes will no longer see and their backs will be bent. I look at my mother's face and memorise the wrinkles on her face. I say in my heart: *I just hope that when I see you next, you'll look just like this*. I start crying, then I hate myself for not controlling my emotions.

I walk towards my father. 'I will probably leave next week.' His eyes light up and he laughs and thanks God for it. 'May you have a good trip,' he says and asks me details about it. I feel that he is faking his happiness.

I tell him that if he wants me to be here, I won't go anywhere. 'No,' he says. 'You should go, you have no future here. Follow your own life and dreams. We will be here, and if fate brings us together, we will see each other again. If not, I send you in the hands of God.' His words break my heart into pieces, and I feel the pain of being a father to a family. I feel again that we never existed: not in the past, present or future.

Winter

8
Zainab's journey

Following the natural codes of secrecy around dangerous travel, the writers usually shared news of their journeys only after they had arrived at the end of them. But in this book, they are placed at the time they took place. Out of a window, Zainab sees the first snow.

Zainab, Kabul

Everywhere was dark in Kabul. I couldn't silence the voices in my head, so I started talking to them.

One of the voices said, *If the Taliban are searching from house to house, they will find you just by asking your name.* I replied, 'I'll give them the wrong name.' The other voice said, *You look like an educated woman. They will notice that and discover the truth.* I replied, 'That's why I borrowed my neighbour's chadar. She has gone to Pakistan herself. I will wear a pair of glasses and pretend I am someone else.'

When a message came through on my phone, the voices stopped. The message was from Dunya.

'Zainab, are you there?'

I haven't known Dunya long. 'Yes. I am here.'

She then sent me a long message with details about a flight to Abu Dhabi. I would need to get to Mazar by 8 p.m. the next day.

I had heard the Taliban tricked people this way and made them disappear. But deep down, I trusted Dunya. With tears of joy, I texted back, 'Yes, thank you.'

She wrote asking me to go to Mazar by bus, with a small bag and travel documents, and to wear something that accorded with the Taliban's rules. When I got to Mazar, I should let her know. 'If, on your journey, someone asks you for a code, your code is BLACK CAT.'

I closed my eyes and decided to listen to the voices again. Now there was a pleasant one. It said, gently, *Didn't you always want to experience a bigger world, see and hear stories of different people, and write them down with the last ink in your pen? So, be brave. Take this step forward.*

When I opened my eyes, there was no sound in my head.

৩০

The women's protests continued in Afghanistan, but with increased suppression, arrests and abductions, they were ever harder to maintain. Zainab and others continued their dissent in subtle ways. Zainab would walk down quiet streets with a can of spray paint, leaving slogans – among them Freedom! and Taliban out! – on walls. Then someone she knew in her neighbourhood joined the Taliban police. He came to her house and threatened her with what he knew. This was when Zainab and her husband decided they needed to leave the country. Zainab does not regret joining the protests. Indeed, the knowledge of having tried to resist the oppression of women in Afghanistan helps her come to terms with what she lost afterwards. She wishes she could have done more.

Zainab's travel out of Afghanistan was also linked to the protests – she was contacted through one of the protesters' WhatsApp groups by a woman she didn't know, who said she would try to help Zainab leave the country.

❧

I woke my husband and shared the news with
him. He said, 'We have lost everything before,
including our homeland. We've already packed
our bags for such a day. There is no other way.'
We agreed that it was time to leave.

In the middle of the night, in empty streets, he
looked for a car. There was no car. Finally, he
called friends for help and located a car. I called
my parents. They and the youngest of my
brothers were awake. I told them how much I
wished to take them with me. 'My heart remains
with you. How can I go?' My mother told me
not to worry and that God is merciful. My
father prayed for us to have a good journey. I

sent kisses to my little sisters, who were asleep, and my sweet-spoken little brother, my tears falling silently.

It was 4 a.m. when we reached the stop for buses to Mazar. We found seats at the back of one. From the moment the bus began to move, my head started to ache. I had always wanted to go to Mazar-e-Sharif on pilgrimage. But now I didn't feel I had the heart or soul to go there.

As soon as we left, I informed Dunya we had set off. She replied, 'When you get close to Mazar, send me a message again.'

The journey from Kabul to Mazar lasted more than eight hours, made longer by the silence of the mountains. We were stuck in Salang Tunnel for over an hour, as traffic in each direction had to pass along a single lane. The scenes around us along the way were natural and poetic, but my exhaustion had stolen all the poetry from the landscape. I saw the season's first snow through the window of the bus. Everywhere felt cold. I didn't know it was also the last snow of my country I was going to see.

I had hidden our documents in a plastic bag under the waistband of my clothes. The bag chafed against my skin. I was sweating and every time I shook myself to get more air, you could hear the crackle of plastic amid the silence of the bus. As soon as we arrived in Mazar, I reached for my phone to text Dunya. Then we heard a voice say the Taliban were going to search inside the bus.

I hid my phone under my clothes too and pulled my headscarf forward. Two Taliba got on to the bus and looked the passengers over. They seemed more interested in the people than the bags. They greeted a few people – an old man on the bus said later that this was to hear their accents. When they reached us, I kept my gaze lowered and tried not to raise the noise of the plastic. One Talib greeted my husband. My husband answered calmly, offering only his Salam in return. After a few minutes they left the bus. I took out my phone. 'I am now in Mazar.'

&

It was about 2 p.m. when we finally got off the bus in Mazar. People climbed into the yellow taxis waiting and soon dispersed. We stood on a corner, and I tried to call a person called Hadi as I'd been instructed by Dunya. But he didn't pick up. Each minute that passed, my anxiety increased. The voices began to criticise me in whispers: *Didn't I tell you this was a trap? You are such a naive girl. Why would anyone on the other side of the world worry about you? The Taliban must have identified you on the bus: as always, reports on the passengers arrive before the passengers themselves.*

Now, the last taxi driver at the station was asking us every minute, 'So where are you going? Can I take you there?' I texted Dunya that there was no news of Hadi. She texted back, 'Wait.' The next moment, she texted me an address and a number with a Belgian dialling code. 'Go to this address. Call Hadi when you get there.'

We shared the address with the driver. It led us to a wedding hall. My headache was severe, it felt like an explosion was going off inside every two seconds. We arrived at the wedding hall, and there was indeed a wedding going on. What kind of a joke was this?

In a state of complete confusion, I texted the Belgian number: 'We've arrived at the wedding hall.' A reply came: 'BLACK CAT, someone is coming to escort you.' I looked around at everyone in their finery, walking around with happy faces. The whole scene gave the impression this part of Afghanistan was not yet subject to the Taliban.

The hall manager saw us and asked us, 'Why are you here?'

I replied, 'I'm looking for someone called Hadi . . . BLACK CAT . . .'

His surprise told me he knew nothing. At that very moment, a man appeared.

'Zainab?'

I confirmed my name.

'Your code?'

'BLACK CAT.'

With a smile, he guided us into the hotel. He was
Hadi. From then on, I trusted him with my life,
for he would be our guide for the rest of our
trip.

ଅ୦

The wedding was going on in one hall. We were
led to another hall and sent to separate male and
female sections. As I entered, I saw a crowd of
women and children. Women and girls sat on
mats along the wall, their legs under blankets.
Children were playing and jumping around in
the corridors, not understanding why they were
there. The hotel staff handed me a mat, a pillow
and a blanket. I sat next to a young girl. The first
thing I did was to remove the plastic bag of
documents from under my clothes. As I wiped
the sweat off it, the girl said, 'Were you told to
come here for the flight as well?'

I smiled at her. 'Yes, is that why you are all here
too?'

She said, 'Yes. My father used to work with
foreigners.'

'Are you travelling with your father?'

'No, sadly, my father was killed. We are going with my brothers.'

My smile faded. 'God bless him, may his place be in Paradise.'

The staff brought me a cup of green tea, something I really needed. My head still ached so much. I tried my best to sleep it off for an hour, but it would have been a miracle to sleep well amid that crowd of children screaming and women gossiping.

When I woke up, I felt dizzy and nauseous. The headache was still there. The crowd in the women's section had grown, there were now mats lined up all the way to the door. Everyone was talking. They say the women's story never ends.

The staff brought dinner. No one minded that we had to gather around *bishqhab kalan*, large plates, and share our meal. I realised that the door was wide open and went to close it. I saw there was no one guarding the door on the other side. I walked further down the corridor to check but there seemed to be no one in charge of protecting this crowd. It woke the voices inside my head. One of them said, *Now you have become an easy morsel for the enemy. These people are not taking care of you. They are your enemy.* The other voice agreed, *That's right, I*

cannot see any sort of protection here either. I
walked back inside the hall and saw the manager
counting plates. He also held a piece of paper
with a list of people. I said, 'Excuse me, how is
the security here?'

Without looking at me, he replied, 'It is very
good. Don't worry.' I wanted to say there is no
one guarding us, and the doors are open. But he
was ordering one of his workers to bring the
teapots.

I returned to my spot to eat my dinner. I ate as if
tomorrow was the start of our important
journey. The voices in my head were calmer now,
until someone brought a message: 'The flight is
delayed. Please be patient.' The food stuck in my
throat. Did it mean there was a problem?

࿇

I realised later that from the moment I started the
bus journey, my fate was not in my hands. I
decided to keep calm and allow events to move me
as if I were a puppet in a play. I observed the crowd
around me. Some had brought suitcases. I spoke to
a woman sitting near me. She was a civil society
activist. I asked about her large case, whether it
would be okay? She replied, 'Well, it's been fine up
to now. Some people have even brought pots and
dishes and heavy curtains.' She looked at my
backpack, which was resting next to my pillow.
'And you, you are so naive, you didn't bring

anything!' I said, 'No, I was just thinking about
surviving, everything else we can get slowly.'

I got distracted by a WhatsApp notification. I
had been added to a group called 'Oranges and
Strawberries' that had eighteen members.
Instead of looking at what was being discussed
in the group, for a moment I thought about
strawberries, their colours and textures. I found
a few men were part of this group too. On the
thread, they shared instructions about our travel.

The first message was that the trip was
postponed until Monday, but we need not
worry, 'There are no serious problems.' Then
there came a cautionary text: 'Do not carry
more than 10,000 US dollars in cash with you
when you arrive at the airport, as it is illegal to
take money out over that limit.' They also
advised those who wished to leave the hotel and
visit families in Mazar, 'You must be back at
the hall by 5 p.m. on Sunday so you are ready
for your early flight on Monday morning.'

I didn't have to think about any of these things.
I did not have even 100 US dollars with me. I
also did not have family in Mazar. So, I stayed
where I was. Before going to bed, I needed to
refresh. I walked to the washrooms. When I got
there, I saw an elderly woman sitting on a bed
in the corridor. I said, 'Salam, are you not cold
here?' She replied, 'No, I prefer it here, close to
washrooms and far from the noise of people.'
Someone came out of the washroom and said

to the woman on the bed, 'Madam Judge, do you need anything?'

Excitedly, I asked, 'Are you a judge?' The elderly woman smiled, confirming she was. I had never met a judge or seen one this close before. 'Are you one of those judges who gives final verdicts?' I knew it was not the right question, but I asked it. 'Did you ever punish criminals? The Taliban?' She said, 'Yes, very often.' I asked again, 'Did any of them ever shed a tear after hearing their verdict? Did you ever feel you'd got it wrong?' With so much confidence, she replied, 'No, we always recognise the criminals. They know themselves too.' The voices in my head smirked. I had not expected this answer. How could we judge anyone so easily? I despaired for a moment.

∞

When I woke up in the morning, I turned on my mobile data. I got a message in the group saying that our location would change from the wedding halls to safe apartments. 'It is only for your safety.'

This sounded like the right decision to me. An apartment would be a much safer and more comfortable place. They had shared pictures of residential apartments and they looked nice. All I wanted was to take a shower.

They had put all the men on floor 8, and floor 9 was reserved for women. Most passengers waited for the lift. Some of us with lighter loads walked up the stairs. When I reached our unit, the door was open. The first room was filled with women and children who had left earlier. Every room was occupied. The voices in my head laughed at me. *Shower? Aren't you taking a shower?* The toilets were already broken, and they kept sending more people into our unit.

I realised that the whole crowd was divided into three or four units. From time to time, the managers would come to the door, and you would see them ask with their eyes, 'How many more people can we fit in here?' But with the protest of the women, they moved along. I realised that the officials here were like any other officials: they showed us a whole building but crammed us into limited rooms. I suspected the trick was to take more money from donors to organise our evacuation, spend little of it and save the rest for themselves. These are the small betrayals people consider clever but led a country to collapse.

Of course, we could endure it: we are Afghans, born to difficult days. But one's heart burns on account of the dishonesty. After a while, the women began asking each other questions and I realised four of them were judges. One of the judges was travelling with her sister. There was also Sarah, who later became my friend, a university professor.

The apartment manager warned us, 'We are no longer responsible for your safety when you step past the apartment door.'

ॐ

That night my husband's friend in Mazar invited us to dinner. We said yes and shared a good meal together. We planned to walk to the holy shrine of Mazar-e-Sharif for a visit the next day. It would be a shame to be in Mazar and not visit its most famous shrine.

At the shrine the next morning, I came face to face with a Talib who said my scarf was not Islamic enough. My husband's friend joined the conversation, to smooth things out and prevent my being questioned further. We returned to the apartment building by 5 p.m.

I had heard that, in Mazar, winters are much colder and summers much warmer than in other provinces. During those two days, I felt the cold weather in my bones. Winter had arrived early. You could even say we had felt cold since the beginning of the year and, in the middle of summer, wintery demons snowed over the heart of the country.

At the apartment gate, I watched some kids playing games and some sitting on the stairs. Youngsters were talking about the politics of America and the role of the Taliban in shaping those politics. Everyone has opinions about the politics of Afghanistan. I stood there listening to all sorts of sounds. After a while, I went inside.

Towards midnight, mothers put their children to bed; they had to be awake for the flight the next morning. We kept getting more messages, being given more instructions:

1. You cannot carry more than 10 kg.
2. Have your ID in hand.
3. Don't carry any kind of weapon, not even knives.
4. Don't carry anything that shows the American flag.
5. Delete all foreign numbers from your notebooks and phones.
6. Clear the chat history of this group.
7. Delete everything from your phone that is considered haram by the Taliban.
8. Don't speak any English.
9. If anyone asks you anything, keep calm and be kind.

There were a few comments and questions about gold and money. The judges – they called each other Qazi Sahib – began to consult with each other. 'Do they weigh gold? I know my bracelets are heavy.' In our room, we tried to sleep in the narrow space available, the children and I more comfortable than the rest. I could hear the counting of paper money. There was a long silence and then the voice of one of the judges. 'I collected this with difficulty, I worked so hard, it is halal, more halal than mother's milk.' One of the voices in my head protested, *Why answer a*

question that has not been asked? I reassured the
voice that God is the real judge. The voice
persisted, *What if these judges took bribes and
released murderers? Now they escape with their
money and the people of Afghanistan remain
with the killers.* 'Maybe you are right,' I shushed
the voice, 'but your suspicion isn't proof.'

Amid this disagreement, a message came through
in the group. 'Dostan-e-aziz, dear friends, tonight
is, most probably, your last night in Afghanistan.'
At once, I felt deeply happy and deeply sad. I was
going to leave my country: my family, my friends
and the people I knew. The warmth and intimacy
I had with them, our house with magical
memories and the mountains that stood around
us like a guard: I was leaving it all behind. The
thing that calmed me were my tears rolling down,
unbidden, to the carpet.

∞

It was about six in the morning when they sent us
a message saying that the flight had been delayed
again. 'Not by much. Don't worry, it is not a
security problem. There is only one more bit of
paperwork to be completed.' I did not understand
what paperwork that could be, but others said
that the foreigners* arranging our travel had to

---

*Zainab's travel out of Afghanistan was facilitated by a US-based charity
set up for the purpose of evacuating people from Afghanistan after the
Taliban takeover placed them at risk. She had only recently been contacted

pay the Taliban 20,000 US dollars for each person on the flight list. Only after the money was paid would we be allowed to fly. I don't know if this was true. The voice inside my head was amazed. *The people who would have been killed so cheaply were sold at a high price.* We were also told the Taliban would remove anyone from the list who was on their own blacklist. Those individuals would either be prevented from flying or would be abducted on the spot.

Finally, around 8.30 a.m., we were told, 'Be ready, you will be taken to the airport on buses.' The coordinators had a list of people on a piece of paper: they would load people on to the buses according to that list. I was shocked to find my name first on the list! The voice laughed at me. *You! Among all these grand personalities!*

It took more than an hour to get everyone loaded on the bus with their luggage. After a few warnings about removing large bags, they sent a message to the group: 'We have more people on our waiting list. If you want your bags to fly, then stay in Mazar yourself! Others are waiting who are ready to travel without a bag!' I could not blame people; they had brought a few bags of their whole life with them and now their hearts and souls were tied to those bags.

---

by the woman who was her original link to the organisation and did not know much about it.

Finally, at 10 a.m., everyone was on the buses and we were ready to leave. The people who had been our representatives up to this point got on the bus and announced themselves to be no one's representative. 'Who says we are representatives? We are not your representatives. Be thoughtful and don't say anything to anyone at the airport. Our business is done here.' They did the same on each of the seven buses. I could smell fear in their words. This fear spread and settled in all of us. They dismounted the bus and the airline representatives introduced themselves. They advised us, 'Please stay calm, there are Taliban checkpoints along the way. They will enter the bus, they may ask you something. You can say very calmly that you have international flights. Try not to be nervous and do not behave suspiciously. This is the first bus: if you play your role well, the buses after yours will also pass without controversy.'

There was no way out now. If we were to be killed at the hands of the Taliban, we were submitting ourselves to them. I was scared, but there was no way to turn back.

৪৩

As the bus moved, the passengers began to pray under their breath. Prayer is our last resort in despair. As the bus moved, my heart was like a fire burning under intense surveillance. I wanted to look out of the window, so that I could come back to my senses, but the driver wouldn't allow it. So, I remained silent and motionless, like someone who, in their last moments, brings the memories of a whole life out for review.

Our bus reached the Taliban checkpoint at the airport. The driver and the representative of the airline got down from the bus and went in the direction of the checkpoint. There was some talk among the passengers. My husband said to me, 'If the situation gets messy, get out of the window and run.'

I shook my head. Deep down, I believed that if the Taliban were to take us away, there would be no way to escape alive. Moments later, a group of armed Taliban entered the bus. They looked at each face carefully. I pulled my scarf down over my eyes.

I raised my head and looked at one Talib for a moment. He looked tall and strong. He was wearing military clothes. His long hair reached his neck and was half tucked into his hat. His forehead was sweaty and his soulless eyes were darkened by kohl. He had lifted his rifle as if ready to shoot. As he glanced at me, I looked down. I kept looking at the floor until our bus passed through the checkpoint and drove into the airport grounds.

We got out of the bus and lined up behind a door. After a moment, the guards let us in. We lined up again where they checked our bags and

sent us through screening. They were looking at
a computer screen and then observed each
person carefully as if they were looking for
someone. The Taliban had women to
interrogate women. One of those women came
out in front of us and showed the man behind
the computer a few photos. 'Have you seen
these?' The man took the pictures and shook his
head. After looking carefully at all the photos,
he turned his gaze to us. Sarah, who was
standing behind me, said, 'I think they are
looking for someone! They are searching for a
woman among us.'

The security guard at the front of our line asked
for my passport. I handed him my *tazkeria*, ID
card. I was scared when he gave my ID to the
man behind the computer. The man looked at it
and then at me. I looked at the airline
representative standing behind him. I made a
questioning face, 'What happened?' The
representative gestured to indicate I should keep
calm. Minutes later, they brought my tazkeria
back and said, 'Put your bag inside the screening
machine.' I was relieved. I was not the person
the Taliban wanted. Slowly, everyone went
through security, and, at last, we found ourselves
in the boarding area.

During the process of checking, there had been a
man with a German shepherd doing the final
security screening. He must have been an official
from the previous government, given the kind of
skilled job he had to do. After we had passed

through, he turned towards us. 'Please, can you help your brother? It's been two months since I received my salary.' My heart ached for the helplessness you could see behind his majestic face. I was completely ashamed of what had been brought between us. We were running away from despair and misery, while he was stuck. We handed him the few thousand Afghanis we had in our pockets. He hugged my husband gratefully and said goodbye.

We stayed in the waiting hall until three in the afternoon. Many passengers changed their clothes: afterwards there were fewer pyjama trousers. Women's black hijabs also disappeared. Everyone's clothes were colourful, and their faces were happy and smiling.

Slowly we climbed up to the aircraft, and everyone took their seats. The plane took off at 4 p.m. I was released. But displaced again: we had lost our homeland. Up in the clouds is a good place to cry and empty the heart.

We arrived in Abu Dhabi that evening and have been living in a camp for Afghan refugees since that night.

Najla, Kabul
Thank God you have left safely, Zainab jan.

Zainab
Thank you, Najla jan.

Masoma, Stockholm, Sweden

May the rest of your journey be good, Zainab jan.

Zainab

Thank you, my dear Masoma. Hope you're doing well.

Marie, Kabul

Safe journey, Zainab jan.

Naeema, Kabul

Have a good journey, Zainab jan.

Najla

Dearest Zainab, have a good journey, stay safe.

Zainab

Thank you all, dear friends. May we all be safe, in the shelter of God, and healthy, happy and calm wherever we go.

In our yard, little grains of snow are falling. The leafless branches have forgotten they belong to a quince tree.

Maryam

9
Winter is coming

1–12 November

Whether at home or as refugees awaiting resettlement, the writers find their lives are suspended. They adapt to the immediate moment and try to find patience within themselves to stay a longer course. Najla reminds her husband they have both lived forty-three years in this state, while Marie flies away from everything she knows, to land in a new world that fascinates her.

Fatima, Herat

Fatima had only one semester more to finish her degree. But in addition to the closures that affect everyone, she faces another problem: if she returns to university, her family becomes more easily traceable. They are trying to keep a low profile, given their former military employment, and are coming to terms with the fact that they may need to leave the country altogether.

We are approaching winter. At this time of the year,
I used to put on my end-of-autumn make-up and
walk to the university with my friend Mariam. We
used to discuss past exams and how to do better in
the next ones. This year, I spend the whole day
staring at the walls of my room. I have no desire to
walk outside. I don't see Mariam any more.

My entire day's task has now become the
embroidery I must finish by the end of the week.

Now, the focus of my life is earning money to
pay for the next day's meal. Three months ago, I
was planning what to study for my master's
degree.

Nilofar, Mazar-e-Sharif

*Alongside her work with NGOs, Nilofar was doing a degree in
Literature, after an earlier degree in Political Science, and was in
her final year when the Taliban took over. After a disrupted
childhood education, she went to school and university as an
adult and her education is a pursuit close to her heart.*

> This is shared pain. My classmates either call or
> text me, asking when they will open the
> university. In the beginning, I kept saying, 'Soon,
> soon, Insh'Allah.' Lately, I have begun to answer
> more tetchily, 'Don't even think about university
> any more. There is no sign of us going to
> university.' Another classmate wrote yesterday to
> ask what I thought about a rumour she'd heard:
> 'They say, they will open universities at the
> beginning of the year, in the month of March.' I
> retorted, 'Why do you ask me if you have this
> news?' She replied, 'It is because you always gave
> us hope.' I felt ashamed.

Naeema, Kabul

Last week a Talib came to our school. There
were many teachers in the school yard, but he
only said Salam to the men and passed all the
ladies. Yesterday, someone told me that he still
doesn't speak to the ladies. So, I insisted on
meeting him. Someone shouted loudly from
inside the office, to be sure I could hear: 'Have

you ever seen me speak to a woman? After all
this time, you want me to speak to a woman?'

Nilofar

Before the fall of the government, a local writers'
group I am part of used to meet on Saturdays to
discuss our stories. With the arrival of the
Taliban, the Department of Culture set a
condition for holding meetings 'without the
presence of women'. No one wanted to attend in
those conditions so, at the suggestion of one of
the professors, they created an online meeting
group instead. This way all the members could
be included.

It is so hard to believe now that people used to
sit and talk and laugh together. But at least
now writers can connect from all over the
world and, most importantly, women can join
from within the four walls of their homes. Who
knew we would go so far back in just a few
months?

Najla, Kabul

*Najla's two youngest daughters would have been in their last
year of school if the Taliban hadn't closed secondary schools for
girls. Najla has sent them to follow a private course instead.*

I was standing in the kitchen. I lifted the lid off
the pot and breathed in the soothing smell of
qoroti with onion, garlic and turmeric. This is
my seven-year-old grandson Mobin's favourite
food. I lowered the flame and covered the pot
again, to keep it warm. The kitchen window was

open, and I could hear the azaan from the mosque. I covered my head and washed the bowls and spoons. I also washed a couple of cucumbers and a few fresh green peppers. I walked down the corridor, glancing at the clock on the wall. I was worried. I said to my husband, 'Our grandchildren are late from school. Why aren't they here yet?'

While I was talking to him, the door opened and the grandchildren walked in. Mobin sniffed the air and sighed contentedly. He smiled at me and suddenly there was a blast. These sounds are nothing new to the children but still, they were frightened. Their faces changed; my heart pounded too. Then we heard gunfire.

We hadn't heard an explosion in weeks.

I reassured the children and invited them to sit for lunch. They gathered around but no one ate with enthusiasm. We heard another explosion and looked at each other.

My heart beat fast. My daughters, Tahmina and Jamila, were at their course in Karte Parwan, a long distance from our place, and they had to change vehicles twice to come home. The road in front of our house is also closed to traffic.

My son, Matin, the father of my grandchildren, wrapped his big scarf around himself and left the house in search of his sisters. His father ran after him to stop him as the shooting was

ongoing, but Matin was gone. My husband
uttered curses under his breath.

Our son came back a few minutes later. He said
the main road was closed to traffic and the
Taliban troops would not allow anyone to cross.

Both my husband and son looked at me. My
husband said, 'We told you the situation was not
good, but you wouldn't listen! Now go and get
your daughters from their course!'

Matin was worried, his face looked distorted. He
said, 'What will we do if the fighting continues
through the night? Call the girls immediately and
tell them not to set off for home.' I called, but
their phones must have been on silent in the class.
I blamed myself for letting them go.

My husband was holding his phone in his hands,
watching the news. He said, 'Look, the BBC
reports a 400-bed hospital in Kabul has been
attacked.' For two hours we listened to the
sound of ambulances. I remembered the
previous attack on this hospital – then
helicopters were in the air, a sound we rarely
hear under this emirati government. I
remembered that during the years of the
republic, helicopters would fly over our block
every day. In an hour, Tahmina and Jamila
would come out of their class.

I asked their father to go in search of them. We
have a small car, but I knew all the roads were

closed. I said, 'Go and bring them back today
and then I'll keep them at home.' Still bitter, he
replied, 'At this time, when no one sends their
sons to their classes, you send these girls!' I
didn't say anything. He left the house, slamming
the door. I prayed that all three would return
home safely.

Because the road leading to the hospital was
blocked, traffic was backed up heavily. I phoned
them back-to-back but none of them answered.
Strange things passed in my mind all afternoon.
My heartache and anxiety kept rising. I listened
to the evening azaan. At that moment, I heard
tapping on the door.

Tahmina does not knock hard on the door when
she comes home, she taps on it slowly with one
finger. So, I knew it was her. I ran to the door.
All three looked tired, their faces sweaty from
walking, even in the cold. I was so happy in my
heart to see them.

Marie, Kabul

I have a flight tomorrow. This whole week, I've
tried to look happy and excited, so that my
parents believe that I'm happy to leave this
country. I don't want to add to their worries. I
tell myself that I must endure the pain of leaving
them here alone and not make their hearts any
heavier. But I packed my suitcase with so much
sadness. A few times, I tried to crack jokes to
break through the sadness in our house. My
mother goes to bed early, saying she has chores

to do early in the morning. I know she goes to her room to cry alone.

Najla

Night came. My grandchildren put their homework back in their bags for the next day. Jamila looked into their room and told them to go to sleep. Tahmina was collecting up cups to bring them to the kitchen for washing. Mobin was still watching the news reports and asking his grandfather questions about the hospital attack. My husband answered some of his questions wearily and then told Mobin not to ask so many questions. Mobin's father believes it is good for the child to know a little bit about the times he's living in so he may know better how to save himself if he gets caught up in trouble.

The grandchildren went to sleep, but the lights were still on in Jamila's and Tahmina's room. Both were studying busily. We live on the main road and cars and tanks passing down the road used to keep us up late, but since the emirati regime took over, it is very quiet. I went to the kitchen to check the taps were properly closed and then I checked the door was locked and the windows fastened as it's already very cold at night.

When I went to my room, my husband was still busy with his phone.

I asked him, 'Will the girls go to their course tomorrow or not?'

He looked up angrily from his screen. 'Did you learn nothing from today's situation?'

I said, 'This situation is not new to me, to you or the girls. You and I have witnessed forty-three years of war in this country.'

'I agree with you, it's a fact.'

'If you agree, then you know that their lessons are invaluable.'

'I also accept this.'

'Then you should also agree it's important they continue their lessons, whatever the circumstances.'

'Only God knows what I went through today, until they were safely home.'

'I do know, but if we stop them going to the course, our situation will be worse: ours and theirs.'

'So, what should we do? God forbid one day they get caught in a bad accident. Tell me what we should do?'

'If we stop them from attending this class, they will be very upset. Being deprived of education is as hard as death.' I said this and pulled the blanket over myself.

Next morning, Tahmina and Jamila left home at 7 a.m. for the course.

∾

Marie

I thought I would start crying when my flight lifted off Afghan soil. But when I saw my country from the tiny window of the plane, probably for the last time, my eyes did not well up. Not even a little bit. I wasn't sad, I wasn't happy either. I felt numb, like a dead body buried nowhere. From the sky, I kept looking at my dried land, my angered land, and began to feel an intense pain within my heart for this lonely landscape. A pain you can't escape or shout out. I reflected on whether my anger had increased since the arrival of the Taliban, but I couldn't tell. As the plane lifted higher and higher into the sky, my feelings melted down and died out. Most of the passengers were crying; why couldn't I?

Fatima

Khuda,[*] God, wants the world to end in
    Afghanistan.
Every day someone is killed,
Every day someone new is arrested.
Our prayers are not heard.

Khuda is a word for God in Persian and numerous other languages/ contexts.

Padaram, my father, wants to sell the house
    he inherited,
To take us to a safe place,
But no one is hopeful enough to buy a
    house.
Watan, homeland: dearest of words, but
    with no hope in it.

Marie, Viersen, Germany

Marie was flown first to Pakistan and ten days later to Germany. She knew very little about her destination. The only place she had ever imagined moving was the UK, because 'the BBC bell' sounded through childhood, when her father listened to its World Service on the radio. To Marie, it was the sound of London. She googled more information about Germany before leaving and asked if she could be sent to Hamburg, but that wasn't possible.

Today is 5 November 2021, which means it has been almost three months since the Taliban took Kabul. As I write this, I am on a bus in Germany. I am not sure I know exactly where they are taking us, but the word 'Düsseldorf' can be seen on the corner of each street we turn onto. I arrived in Germany last night, around eight o'clock, after a thirteen-hour flight. My legs still feel numb, my ears are still ringing from all the crying babies on the flight.

I used to work with Germans in Kabul. When the situation got worse, the office decided to transfer its employees to Germany. We are out of our cursed land, but I don't feel happy. Others around me are very happy. They are laughing, telling jokes and talking about the future. But not me. When I look inwards, I find myself completely cold and emotionless. I don't have butterflies in my stomach. I've tried to be happy, but nothing lifts my heart.

Every time I try to think about what I should do here, my family comes to my mind and I feel bitter about everything. I remember my mother's eyes as she tried to hide her sadness; my father's trembling hands as he said goodbye. My sister and my brother didn't say anything at all, but I understood what they wanted to say. All of these thoughts and feelings are driving me crazy.

Marie

Today is 6 November and it's my birthday. It is my first full day in Germany. To be born on this day and start a new life on this day is an interesting coincidence. I congratulated myself in this place where I've started a lonely life. After that, I checked my messages on all social media. My mother had sent me a photo of a cake with Happy Birthday written on it. I was both happy and sad. I prayed we would be together again in time – safe, healthy and happy – and that we should never become refugees again. I didn't wish for anything else. A silent and blindfolded birth.

Fatima

I am also going to leave next week,
I don't know how to pack my things.

What to take? Notebooks and pens?
Or my winter clothes?

It is different this time.
I am becoming a refugee.

I am leaving my homeland and I won't return,
Going in search of safety and a quiet life,
But where in the world I don't yet know.

Freshta, Dushanbe, Tajikistan

I am like a shadow that is always lost in others.
Today I learned the Tajik government does not
recognise the new Afghan regime, so they aren't
issuing visas to anyone and won't extend old
visas. I respect their politics and law, but I cried
because we became unrelated. No one recognises
us and we don't get to live peacefully anywhere.

Zainab, Abu Dhabi, UAE

The refugees say that this Abu Dhabi camp
where we are staying, the Emirates Humanitarian
City, used to be a military camp. That's why it
has an alarm system and iron gates that look like
they've been armoured. No one has a key for
locking any door here, so everyone is always
available. This has already caused controversy.

The young men play and walk in the parks past
midnight. One midnight, there were some
people playing volleyball noisily, and one of the
residents in Block E4 poured water on their
heads. Among the volleyball players was a
wicked young man with long hair, whom many

girls had complained about. He went up to the
third floor to look for the person who threw the
water. He had to enter many rooms before he
found them. But then he got beaten up by several
other men, who said that he had entered their
rooms when their women were not covered.
There was an uproar for several hours that
night.

The Arabs visit us sometimes, but only to
resolve our issues. The people who work here are
from Pakistan, India and Bangladesh.

Another night, the alarm went off. It was
deafening. We all got up thinking there was war
or a fire or something like that. We found it was
just a man who had smoked a cigarette in the
no-smoking zone. As if he wanted to smoke his
life away in the middle of the night.

Each room has only one small window,
double-glazed, its material seemingly
unbreakable. We cannot open it fully, so no
one can throw themselves down. Neither with
the intention of suicide, nor the intention of
escaping.

We were put into quarantine on arriving here. I
don't understand why we have to live like this.
We escaped the danger of the Taliban and left
everything behind, only to be imprisoned here. It
is maddening. If anyone would throw herself out
of this window, it would be for freedom.

We are in block A3, room 302, in a three-by-nine-metre white room with two beds, a small wardrobe and a small desk. The bathroom and toilet are along one side of the room. All of the rooms are the same size and have paper-thin walls. They all look the same, room after room, block after block. I've been feeling restless, I want to go outside. I need fresh air to breathe. I just want to go outside. That is the only thing that would make me feel better. I think I now know what it feels like to be imprisoned.

There are doctors and nurses here.

One of the doctors asked me, 'Do you feel any unhappiness or depression?'

'Why do you ask?'

'About leaving your country, your family . . .'

I said, 'No . . .'

Then my tears started falling. In reality, I do not know how I am doing.

℘

Freshta

The sun shone brightly this morning. My heart told me today I might hear some good news. I put on my formal clothes. I wanted to wear my thin coat, but the weather is colder now, so I wore my heavy coat. I left home with many hopes. I had heard recently that the UN office helps journalists and young people to apply for asylum in the United States and Canada.

When I arrived at the UN office, I saw two luxury cars parked outside with the UNHCR logo on them, but the office door was closed. I knocked but there was no response. I noticed a bell and pressed it and a man popped his head out of a small window. 'What do you want?'

'Sir, I am Freshta ——, I am an Afghan journalist and writer. I would like to speak with your boss or any other staff.'

He replied sharply, 'Whether you're a reporter or whoever, it's Covid, neither the director nor anyone else will see you.' I asked if he could give me a phone number or email address. 'No, no,' he said, closing the window.

All the way home, I kept wondering what this office is for. Will they not even listen to the problems of the refugees? These last two years we have received neither financial support nor moral support.

I was depressed and angry. Leaves were falling everywhere but I couldn't locate my old love for them.

In Tajikistan, Freshta rarely mentions that she is a writer, so as not to invite scrutiny. She and her husband are both journalists and sorely miss their old work. Back in Afghanistan, Freshta reported on issues such as women's custody rights over their children after separation, or women facing violence from former husbands.

Marie

I am in a city called Viersen. It is a beautiful city: it has beautiful houses with flowers in vases at little windows. Tall trees in red and yellow lift the weariness from the city; the footpaths are piled with fallen leaves that look like rainbows on the ground. To find the cycle routes, you have to clear the leaves and say hello to passers-by. On sunny days, the city looks like a newlywed bride under the blue sky, bringing comfort to the eye.

There is a small shop near a corner of the river where ducks graze in groups. The shop owner is a well-dressed and friendly old man. He can speak English. The other day, I went inside and asked for a coffee, and he gave me a coffee with a nice smile.

On the horizon, you can see a green hill with many trees that look like pine or oak. I walk towards the hill; I want to walk without any need to stop. It reminds me of my childhood. I remember a cartoon drama called *Story of the Alps: My Annette*. In it, the character Lucien Morel transforms his loneliness and anger by making wooden tools in the wilderness. He always returns home happy and content. Now, I

think I'd like to walk up that hill and into the
forest.

When I was a child, I wanted to experience the
life such people lived on hills, in forests, in
single-storey houses and on big roads. Now that
I am here in the green places of Europe, I
remember those wishes of my childhood and I
am happy that I had such a childhood. I close
my eyes and I feel like I am Lucien in the
wilderness, fighting fear and loneliness. For a
moment, despite all the difficult days, this makes
me happy.

10
Jagged everydays
12 November–31 December

In Afghanistan, daily life is difficult. Prices have gone up. The Taliban insist on women having a mahram, a male chaperone from their family, to accompany them on every journey out of their homes. The writers try to resist these restrictions, but they are also fed up.*

Farangis, San Francisco, USA

Farangis has been in San Francisco since the time of Kabul's fall. She arrived heavily pregnant on an evacuation flight; afterwards she read of two women who had given birth on their flights. She worries constantly about her family back in Afghanistan.

As time passes, I become even more anxious. I talked to my mother in Afghanistan last night She told me the cost of living has increased dramatically. My brother lost his job when the Taliban took over the government and he's currently unemployed. A can of oil used to cost 400 Afghani but now it is 1,200. My mother says they can't afford to buy food at these prices. I

---

*According to the Taliban rule – although it is not consistently articulated or applied – a woman needs to be accompanied in public by a close male relative, such as a father, brother, husband or son. This male relative is considered the woman's 'guardian' and is also responsible for her adherence to Taliban rules of dress, etc.

am very worried about my family. On one side
there is the security problem; on the other,
unemployment and poverty.

Nilofar, Mazar-e-Sharif

Today I saw on Facebook that the Taliban in
Herat are troubling women who appear alone on
the roads and in taxis. I'm so terrified. If this
starts happening here, how am I going to go
outside? My brother can't accompany me all the
time. I remember the images from thirty years
ago when the Taliban beat women with their
shalaaq, whips, and women trembled on the
floor in their blue burqas. We are going back to
that time. I am still shocked that this is
happening.

Farangis

Yesterday, I read on Facebook that the Taliban
ordered drivers not to allow women without
mahrams into their cars. My sister is a doctor,
and she goes to the hospital alone every day.
What will she do now? How will she continue
her job?

Parand, Kabul

*Parand perseveres, going to work, despite new sources of strain.
The Taliban have summoned her husband to report to one of
their stations in Kabul, but he hasn't followed their order. The
couple are also under threat from relatives, who disapprove of
their marriage across ethnic groups. They live in relative secrecy,
not appearing much together and trying not to be noticed by the
neighbours. They have not been married long.*

The room above has recently been rented out to a family with two young daughters. Since their arrival, it seems like a dead house has come back to life, their voices refracting through the walls. One of the girls is ten years old and the other is seven. They are full of talk and joy, like sparrows, and I enjoy listening in. In the afternoons, they play together and act out different roles. Today, one was a schoolgirl and the other a Talib. The schoolgirl screamed and begged not to be hit. But the Talib would not consider non-violence. 'Your dress is too short, why don't you have a scarf? And why did you come to school without our permission?' Hearing this, I was overwhelmed with gloomy thoughts. All I could think was how this horror has already spread into all parts of our lives and eaten our spirits like termites do. Even children are not spared.

Nilofar

This is so bad. The Taliban are already present in our children's games!

Parand

Sadly yes. I used to worry on the roads about getting caught up in an explosion. Now another distress has been added. On my way to work, there are checkpoints every hundred metres. Every time the office car approaches a group of Taliban, my heart beats like broken glass. I'm so afraid they'll reprimand me for my clothes or pull me out of the car for travelling with male colleagues. Or worse, start interrogating my office about what I do there.

Nilofar

Oh yes. When, on top of that, they start
insisting we must have a mahram with us, what
will we do then?

> **Parand**
>
> We are still experiencing the calm before the
> storm.
>
> **Parand**
>
> We've started going to the office without official
> permission.

Nilofar

I personally don't have any mahram. I only have
one brother, and he has a job. So, I'm not eligible
for the jobs being advertised – they announce
during the interview process that a mahram is a
'must-have'.

> **Parand**
>
> Elsewhere in the world, women have gone to
> space. Look at us, worrying about whether we
> have a male relative to accompany us. What a
> shop the Taliban run: selling religious rules and
> regulations for their own profit.

Nilofar

I swear these people are doing business in the
name of religion. Where are those people now
who used to say that during the time of Caliph

Umar,* women could travel safely alone from
Baghdad to Mecca, even wearing golden crowns?
We can't even go to the next province. Every day
I am more and more concerned about the future.

Parand

These days, my heart is in the grip of grief.
Whenever I eat or I find myself in a warm room,
I feel guilty. I am ashamed that I am comfortable
and have food to eat, while many of my
compatriots cannot sleep, their rooms cold and
their stomachs empty. So many children are on
the streets begging. Everyone is terrified of
inflation – the currency falls, and the prices of
fuel and food keep going up. Unemployment
adds to everyone's troubles. Today, on the bus,
everyone was talking about rising prices. A
woman at the back said she would prefer if
doomsday came to end this situation. She kept
saying, 'This inflation, the incomparable cold of
this winter, then on top of that my husband and
I are both out of work. Sometimes, I just want
to gather all my children in one room and set fire
to that room.' I don't know any more why we
are all burning in this fire, and at whose hand.
Soon we will turn to ash.

Nilofar

These days, I do embroidery. I used to be a person
who never wanted to do such things. But now
when I focus on weaving and counting threads

---

*Caliph Umar ibn al-Khattab was the second caliph of Islam. He ruled
from 634 to 644.

and needles, I am less stressed. At least, when I'm
busy sewing, I don't think about anything
gloomy, and that's good. It has helped me.

Farangis

I cannot bear the fact that I have come to a safe
place, but my family still lives in a land with no
future.

A few days ago, I sent some money to my
mother. My brother went to the bank to
withdraw the money, but he couldn't, because
the bank was too crowded. The next day my
brother went back to the bank at 3 a.m. and was
finally able to take the money out at 9 a.m.

Nilofar

My recent worries are all about the Taliban
arresting former military personnel. The
military leaders were able to leave, but the
ordinary foot soldiers, who followed their
orders, are being sacrificed every day. Thoughts
of their unemployment on the one hand and the
news of their arrests on the other torment me. I
wish this nightmare would end.

Parand

The Taliban have put my husband on their list
for arrest. There seems to be no escape for us.
Every time there is a knock on the door, I die a
thousand times, thinking that they've come to
take him. Other people are suffering from
hunger. You can only ignore such a situation if
you are a stone. In the city, our circle of freedom

shrinks every day. There is no hope for the future. Every day, they announce a new commandment to tie our hands and feet.

ಬಿ

Najla

It was about 11 a.m. I went in through the eastern door of the park. I looked up at the patchy clouds in a hot sky and at the people milling around. Most of the men in Kabul who used to wear jeans or trousers now wear traditional *shalwar kamiz*. I saw two boys dressed traditionally, with short beards. They were wearing trainers and they looked affluent and educated – chatting while showing each other things on their mobile phones.

I passed by them and went to the area where four benches are placed around a table. This area is usually used only by the ladies, and it was full today. I took the one space left and said Salam. A young woman welcomed me to the group there.

An older woman was fixing her white headscarf over her dyed black hair. She said, 'Thank God, we have a balcony where the sun shines, but what can I do? I feel depressed at home and come to the park to meet other people and change my mood.' Another woman wiped the corners of her lips with her fingers and said,

'You do the right thing. I also feel depressed at home. Our flat doesn't get much sunlight. I have pain in my bones and the doctor advised me to sit in sunshine.'

Another woman, the oldest present, said, 'I am afraid of the day the Taliban stop us coming to these parks.' A fifth woman, with thin pencilled eyebrows, joined in the conversation, 'There is no doubt they will prevent us coming to the park. They have only just begun with their circus show.' The oldest woman said, 'God forbid.' The rest of the ladies chorused, 'Ameen.'

The woman with the white scarf said, 'I hope the Taliban do not hear us.' The young woman who first greeted me was restless. She said, 'Since the Taliban came, I am apprehensive. My son was in his fourth year of university. He hasn't been out since that day – this is the first time he's getting fresh air or sunshine. I hope the Taliban don't come here.' I thought perhaps she was talking about the boys I saw when I entered the park.

At that very moment, two armed Taliba entered the park. The young woman became even more restless and as I looked back, I saw that the Taliban had apprehended the two boys I saw earlier. The woman in the white scarf said to the young woman, 'Look around quickly, is your son one of those they've taken?' The young woman ran, her headscarf falling off and her handbag still on the bench. She pushed the Talib and grabbed her son's hand. She looked petrified. She shouted at the Talib, 'Leave my son alone. He's done nothing. Where are you taking him?' The Talib pushed her away and they took the boys out of the park. The mother fainted. I ran to her, gave her back her headscarf and helped her stand up. She wept and regretted ever bringing her son out of the house.

A tall man came towards us and said, 'Don't worry, they will release your son soon. They only check their mobile phones.'

'Why?'

'They check the mobile phones to see if the person has photos of former army officers or anything critical of the Taliban regime. This is now common knowledge but maybe your son did not know it.'

The man then sighed and looked around apprehensively, in case a Talib saw him speaking with women.

'Every day the Taliban take three or four people with mobile phones. Many young men do not carry their mobile phones out with them any more. I know it is very personal to look into a person's phone, but the Taliban don't understand this or else they do it deliberately.'

ᘓ

Zainab, Abu Dhabi, UAE

After a crisis, when you start living more
normally, you realise you've forgotten to bring
small and essential things with you.
Inconsequential things like nail clippers, a needle
and thread, tweezers, a comb. I start to think
about how to repurpose what I do have. One
day, as I was eating some chicken with a
disposable knife and a fork, I realised how useful
a fork could be. I washed my fork very clean and
started combing my hair with it that evening. I
broke two forks, but my hair was nicely combed.

But then there are things that can never be
replaced, like having a clear glass cup to drink tea
in, instead of taking your tea with the smell of a
paper cup. I remember seeing people carrying their
teapots and kettles and most probably their cups
with them on the journey here. I've known since
then how important our tea is to us. Those people
now share their kettles, and we rely on them to
grant us the best cardamom tea here.

Maryam, Kabul

Zainab jan, I've been following your story so far.
I don't have regular electricity or internet, but I
can't wait to read the next instalments. Good
luck, my dear.

Maryam

And Ms Parand jan, please be careful. I was so
happy to know that you are still going to your
office, and I want to congratulate you on your

bravery. Honestly, I would be too scared. Whenever I leave the house, I am very anxious all the way. I wish you good health and safety.

Zainab

Love you, Maryam jan. I try to write about my experiences every night so I can share them with you all. I still have so much to say. For now, take care of yourselves.

Parand

Thank you, Maryam jan. At this time, our days are indescribable.

Where the writers are

31 December 2021

As the year turns from 2021 to 2022, only seven of the writers are still in Afghanistan. Freshta was already living in Tajikistan, and Fakhta and Fatima have been smuggled to Iran, where Elahe has always lived. Many of the other writers are living in temporary refugee camps, their expected lengths of stay unknown. The group is now in conversation across twelve countries and seven time zones.

In Afghanistan:

Atifa

Atifa remains in Herat, Afghanistan, living with her widowed mother, her sisters and the youngest of her brothers.

Maryam

Maryam remains at home in Kabul. She continues to read the diary but sometimes cannot do it for the heartbreak. After a few difficult months, she has decided to start writing letters to Beethoven. She has been listening to his music and feels he might understand her, since he also struggled with his health. She has only personal, intimate details of her days to share and needs someone to hear them.

Naeema

Naeema continues to work as a teacher, living in Kabul with her sister, her brother and her brother's family.

Najla

Najla remains in Kabul, though she discusses with her husband whether the family should leave for the sake of the children and grandchildren.

Nilofar

Nilofar wishes to leave Afghanistan with her brother and sister but remains in the northern city of Mazar-e-Sharif.

Parand

Parand and her husband have tried living in both Kabul and Kunduz since the fall, on account of the threat to her husband's safety. Neither is a perfect haven but Parand is glad she is able to escape the city into landscapes that nourish her.

Sadaf

Sadaf remains in Kabul, still working as a teacher when schools are open.

In the immediate region.

Elahe

Elahe remains in Iran, where she and her family have been refugees since the 1980s. For more than thirty years, their documentation in Iran took the form of cards that declared them Afghan refugees. They now hold residence cards with restrictions.

Fakhta

Fakhta and her husband took a loan from relatives to pay a smuggler to escort them from Herat across the border to Iran. They have made it to a village outside Tehran and are living with other extended family while they look for a place to live. Fakhta's husband goes out to work on construction sites, while Fakhta does occasional work in the fields. They are both paid by the day.

Fatima

Fatima and her parents also travelled to Iran over the land border in late December. They passed through Mashhad to settle in Semnan in central Iran. It is a big and developed city, Fatima says, in which you need a bank card for everything, even to visit a doctor. This is a challenge, because as refugees they are not permitted to hold bank accounts.

Freshta

Freshta and her husband are still living in Dushanbe, Tajikistan, still hoping to be accepted for resettlement in another country.

In the Middle East and Europe:

Batool

One day, Batool realised a video in which she talked about her research into paedophilia had been circulating online. She clicked on an old link to discover it had been viewed 4 million times. She worried this publicity could bring her to the attention of the Taliban. Batool and her husband decided the level of risk was now too high and they must try to leave the country. They wanted to go back to Iran, but by now the border was closed. They made their way to Pakistan, whipped by the Taliban on their way out of the country. Then a journalist in Italy – someone Batool didn't know but had been in touch with by email – managed to arrange for the family to be flown to Rome. It was late November when they landed; Batool remembers Christmas was coming.

Marie

Marie arrived in Germany at the start of November and has been resettled in a town called Bad-Berleburg. She goes daily to German-language classes. She already speaks Dari, English and some Urdu/Hindi, but says in none of those languages do you need to know if an orange is male or female.

Masoma

Masoma's two-month journey of escape ended in Stockholm, Sweden, which she had been told was a good country for single women.

Nora

Three weeks after their first abortive journey to the airport in late August, Nora and her husband and children managed to travel to Pakistan and from there to their approved destination in Spain – for which they had paperwork on account of her husband's previous work. They had only ever travelled on holiday before, and Nora says it was during their first night in Madrid that she realised what it meant to be a refugee. They live confined in a camp where they have to ask permission to do anything at all. While there are opportunities for women to learn beauty trades or cleaning skills, she has been told her medical qualifications are unlikely to be accepted in Spain.

Samira

Samira spent three days inside Kabul airport before she was able to board a military plane to Dubai. Her husband had been living in France for five years, as an Amazon delivery driver, and with the help of his local mayor was able to make an official request to the French government to have Samira evacuated from Kabul and brought to France. From Dubai she flew on to Paris and was reunited with her husband, to start a new life in Bordeaux. Every day, she reads terrible news from Afghanistan, where the rest of her family remains.

Zainab

Zainab is living with her husband among other Afghan refugees in the Emirates Humanitarian City just outside Abu Dhabi, UAE. They are awaiting resettlement in a new country.

Across the Atlantic Ocean:

Farangis

Farangis is in San Francisco, where she has lived before. At first, she and her husband stayed with her sister-in-law, who already lived there, but gradually set up house by themselves. Their son was born a week after they arrived in America.

Farishta

With the help of the US Embassy, Farishta and her family were escorted to the airport by Afghan troops within a fortnight of the fall of Kabul. She knew how lucky they were, but at the airport couldn't hold back her tears at leaving her homeland. A soldier saw her crying and told her not to, that he still carried a hope they could return one day. Farishta and her mother and sisters travelled to a refugee camp in Bahrain, where her brother joined them, flying in directly from his medical school in Russia. They were flown to a refugee camp in Italy and finally to a camp in New Jersey, USA. Here the family separated again: Farishta's brother, her married sisters, brothers-in-law and one other sister stayed in the US, while Farishta, her mother and one sister went on to Ottawa, Canada.

Mehrsa

Mehrsa is still on her master's course in Women's and Gender Studies in Iowa, USA. She is not very comfortable in Cedar Falls, where she is located, but the course keeps her going because it is so interesting and makes her feel her life matters. She has also joined creative writing classes.

In the Pacific:

Rana

In late November, Rana was teaching when she received a call from her mother telling her to come home as the family planned to leave Afghanistan the same day. Rana had to leave without saying proper goodbyes to her colleagues. That night she, her mother, two brothers, a sister-in-law and two nieces drove to the border with Pakistan, making a frightening journey in darkness because it was said the Taliban didn't search cars at night. There were thousands of people at the border, Rana said, and they struggled to get their clearance to enter Pakistan. They made their way to Islamabad and a week later they were flown to Brisbane by the Australian government. As the year turns, they've just completed a two-week Covid quarantine in a hotel in Brisbane and chosen Melbourne as the city in which they would like to be resettled.

According to the Hijri/Shamsi calendar followed in Afghanistan, the new year will not come till Nowruz, on the first day of spring. A long winter is still unfolding.

2022

We are surrounded by snow. The hands of the quince tree are frozen. It has no shelter from this cold. And neither do we, from poverty, desperation and oppression across the country.

Maryam

11
Fear and snow
1–12 January

Masoma, Stockholm, Sweden

Today is the first day of the year and my eyes are
like a cloudy sky on the verge of rain. My heart
is full of pain and the world feels like a prison to
me. I just want to get away from it all.

Fatima, Semnan, Iran

To leave our home and our relatives did not seem
a difficult decision until we arrived at the border
with Iran. Perhaps I will never return.

Parand, Kabul

I am looking out of the window. It is snowing
steadily, piling up on the ground. In other years,
we would jump for joy and spend hours watching
snowflakes falling through the air. Today, I don't
have the patience. These are not happy days for
me. I've lost my self-confidence and the
motivation to do anything at all. I used to make
comical sketches and write jokes to cheer myself
up. Now, my faith is broken, and I keep asking
myself questions. When will everything be fine?
Why did we end up in this situation? How long
will this regime use us women as a tool? Don't
these governments in Afghanistan know any way
to promote themselves apart from the way they

inflict themselves on women? Can't they leave us
to breathe?

&

Najla, Kabul

This week, when my grandson Mobin came home,
I asked him about school. I was worried because,
with the establishment of the Taliban emirate, the
situation has become more frightening.

Mobin is seven. He said to me confidently, 'I'm
not scared. I'm not small any more. Sometimes
you tell me I'm a big man.'

I replied, 'Thank God you are all grown up.
There are dogs on the way, that's why I asked.'

Last week, I was told that a green ranger vehicle
was parked in front of the school gate with
several Taliban soldiers around it. Mobin said,
'Other kids are afraid of it, but I am not afraid.'

I was sad. Armed men standing in front of a school
seemed strange to me. In the past, although the
security situation was worse – with the republic
under attack from the Taliban and others – there
was nothing like this. I assured Mobin the armed
guards didn't have anything to do with him.

One afternoon, I stood near the window and
watched for Mobin's arrival. I would usually
catch his eye out of the window, but today he

didn't see me. He ran in and slammed the door
with his little hands. I saw Mobin throw his
schoolbag to the floor in the hallway and enter
the bathroom with his shoes on.

He shut the bathroom door. From the other side,
I asked, 'Dearest child, are you okay?'

He replied, hoarsely: 'I'm fine!'

'Thank God you are fine. I was worried. Wash
your hands with soap and water.'

I turned back towards the kitchen when Mobin
exclaimed from the toilet: '*Anaa*, Grandma!' He
knocked on the bathroom door and said, 'Give
me my house clothes!'

'You can change when you come out.' He cried
out that he couldn't.

I got his clothes from the closet, and he opened
the door partway to take them. After he came
out, I went into the bathroom and saw his
pants and shoes in a corner. I lifted his pants
with two fingers of my left hand and brought
them up to my nose. I realised what had
happened, but I wondered why, when there are
so many toilets at the school. When I came out
of the bathroom, I acted like I hadn't seen
anything. We had our lunch, then I filled the
big kettle with water and connected it to the
electricity. I washed Mobin's pants and shoes
and hung them from the window of the back

porch where Mobin wouldn't see them. I filled
two cups of tea and put a few chocolates beside
them on a plate. I invited Mobin to come and
sit with me.

'Anaa! Do you know who came to our school
today?'

'No dear, how would I know? I've been sitting at
home all day!'

'Taliban came. They had guns on their
shoulders.'

'Oh.'

'Before they came to our class, our teacher left
the classroom.'

'She would have been told that the Taliban were
coming.'

'I don't know. It's good she wasn't in the
classroom, or she would have been very scared.'

'The teachers are not scared, baby.'

'How do you know?'

'When people grow up, they don't get scared.'

'I'm big too, I'm not afraid, but the Taliban are
bigger than me.'

'Tell me what happened next?'

'One Talib asked us to read our lesson.'

'What did you answer?'

'Everyone was silent, no one answered.'

'And then?'

'Then he pulled the gun off his shoulder and startled us.'

My heart pounded. 'And then what did he do? He didn't shoot?'

'No, he didn't shoot, but we were all scared. We thought he'd hit us with the machine gun. He didn't. But he told us, *If you don't study, we will kill you.*'

I drew Mobin closer to me and put my arm around his shoulder. He was silent for a few moments. Then he wriggled away from my arm. He peeled the wrapper off a chocolate and put it in his mouth. 'Anaa, when you were in school, did the Taliban come to your class?'

'No, they did not exist at that time.'

I let out a cold breath and leaned back against the cushion.

৯০

Parand

Wherever you go, no good news is waiting for you.
I learned today that the bathkeeper's daughter is
engaged. She is about to enter Year 7, she is
thirteen years old. Her mother keeps saying that
school will never start, let her follow her *bakht*,
her fortune, in her husband's home. It is numbing.

This little girl's situation reminds me of my own
during the first Taliban regime. I faced so much
hopelessness and disappointment and ended up in
an unsuccessful marriage. I suffered so much. The
wounds and injuries of my first marriage still
haven't healed. Every night, I have nightmares
about being rejected, humiliated and considered
worthless. Yet I rose from those ashes and stood
on my own feet. Will this girl and hundreds of
other girls who are victims of this situation ever
have the chance to find themselves again?

*The early years of Parand's childhood were peaceful. Her parents
were government employees and they lived in a nice house with
a garden. That's all she remembers before life was disrupted by
the mujahideen wars.* Schools were often closed in the years

---

*The mujahideen in the context of Afghan history refers to a multitude of
individual militia groups as well as a loose coalition formed of these groups
in 1979 to resist the Soviet invasion. After the Soviets withdrew in 1989,
rival factions fell out and fought each other. Between 1992 and 1996, Kabul
was controlled by successive mujahideen groups and power-sharing
arrangements and decimated by fighting between them. When the Taliban
established control over Afghanistan's government in 1996, mujahideen
militias continued to fight against their control, a coalition called the
Northern Alliance emerging as the strongest force against the Taliban.

after, and when the Taliban came – Parand was fourteen – they closed altogether to girls. Many girls stuck at home were given in underage marriages, many parents feeling their daughters would be safer married than vulnerable to predatory warlords. Parand was one of them.

Her first marriage was a terrible experience. She found herself in a very conservative family – even after the departure of the Taliban, she struggled to convince the family to let her go to school. She sat at home for six years, but finally managed to go back, finishing secondary school at twenty-nine. Further education seemed out of the question, but Parand managed to get one of her brothers-in-law, visiting from abroad, to persuade his family to let her go to university. They agreed but spent the next few years judging and hectoring Parand, telling her how to dress and how to behave. As she approached graduation, now capable of more independence, they began to threaten her more violently. They stopped her going to university altogether. This was when Parand sought support from one of her own brothers to help her separate from her husband. The divorce took longer than it need have, because Parand's husband would not attend the court dates, but she returned to live at her parents' house and did get her divorce after two years. She needed to support herself now and for another two years she struggled to find a job – running into misogyny and nepotism everywhere – before she was recruited to the job she works in now.

Farangis, San Francisco, USA

Today, my son is four months old. He knows me now. He is happy when I am with him because he knows I only wish him goodness, that I am here to take care of him and fulfil his small

---

Militia groups fighting the Taliban were also supported by the US throughout the American invasion of Afghanistan to prevent the Taliban from gaining territory.

wishes. I remember the day he was born: it was not easy, not at all easy. During my labour, I thought about my family, especially my dear mother. I kept reading news about Afghanistan. Even in labour, I was more worried about my family back home. The pain of childbirth was not as intense as the pain in my heart for them.

Farangis's son was born a week after the fall of Kabul and a week after she and her husband arrived in America. She missed her mother especially at the birth of her child. It was her first time with a baby and her husband's too, she says. In the initial months, they would rush to the hospital when they couldn't work out why the baby was crying.

Najla

I went to my brother's house. Behlol is my nephew. I saw him reading his books and trying to finish his homework. At one point, he looked at his wristwatch, collected up his books and notebooks and called out to his mother that he was off to his English course. He is ten years old, a strong boy with pale skin and red cheeks that make him even more handsome.

After Behlol set off, his mother, Humaira, told me a story. One day, when Behlol returned home, he said there had been a green car on the roadside that belonged to the Taliban. Someone had called to him from the vehicle, but Behlol didn't want to go near him. He was scared. The Talib shouted again and Behlol approached, but he was shaking with fear. The Talib asked:

'Where have you been?'

'I went to the course.'

'What course?'

'English and Maths.'

'You are the son of an Englishman?'

'No, I am Afghan.'

'Why were you looking at our car? Can you show me what is in your pockets?'

'It would be best if you did not touch my pockets.'

'I want to see what is in there.'

'There is nothing.'

The Talib put his hand in Behlol's pocket and took out a green pencil, a blue pen and a red eraser. Behlol wanted them back. The Talib returned his belongings and said, 'Go now and don't come back this way again.'

The next day Behlol did not go to his course. He hadn't told his mother the story and Humaira couldn't work out what had happened to her son all of a sudden. Behlol finally told her what had happened the day before. Humaira insisted he should not be cowed. She told him the Taliban

wanted to scare him so he wouldn't go to school
and he and his generation would remain illiterate.

Behlol agreed with her logic but wondered what
route he could use to avoid the Taliban. Then he
remembered the basement door, through which
he could slip out unnoticed. Down there he also
found his old schoolbag and many other bits
and pieces in storage. He now goes to his course
in a different disguise each day. His mother
watches as he walks out in his grandfather's
sunglasses, turning to smile and wave at her.

Freshta, Dushanbe, Tajikistan

After a long day, I entered the bakery. A kind Tajik
woman owns it. She always smiles and you can see
in her face that she works because she must, even
though she is elderly and always looks tired. She
says she has grandchildren, but they all have their
own houses. She and one daughter live alone, so
she works from morning to night. I'm glad she is
able to work and not go begging to others.

But yesterday she said something that still
disturbs me. I entered the bakery to buy some
cookies, and she looked at my pregnant belly
and asked, 'How old is the baby you are
carrying?' I said, 'This is my eighth month,
thank God.'

She asked, 'Son or daughter?' I told her the
doctor said it was a girl. The woman sighed
coldly to show her heart was sad for me. 'Don't
worry, the next will be a boy.'

I asked myself: is it an animal growing inside me that people react like this? I was so hopeful the doctor would say it was a girl, because I so wanted a daughter. But this is not the first time I have seen such a reaction. And the most painful thing is that these reactions come from women.

Freshta is one of eight daughters.

&

Najla

I was peeling boiled potatoes. Mobin ran into the kitchen and stretched his little hand towards the window.

'Anaa, look outside! The whole earth is covered with snow.'

The hot potatoes had steamed up the kitchen window. I wiped the glass and looked outside. Snow was falling and the ground was white. There were white lines along the branches and power lines.

I turned to Mobin and said, 'After many years of drought, this year we seem to be prosperous.'

He asked me, 'What good will it do if it snows?'

'If there is a lot of snow and rain, the rivers will be full of water. Groundwater will increase.'

'What else?'

'Farmers will plant their fields in the spring and get a good harvest in the summer. There will be plenty of fruit and grain in the markets.'

'Farmers don't like to lose anything, do they – like you and me?'

It reminded me of the day I told him not to take anything from anyone. I told him the giving hand is better than the receiving hand. I said then, 'My child, the good life is when someone works hard, trusts in their own hands and doesn't need anyone.' At the time, he replied, 'Grandma, I want to do everything on my own.'

'Anaa, now tell me another benefit of the snow.'

I thought for a moment and said: 'You tell me.'

He smiled. 'You don't know this one, but I do. It's that we can make a snowman.' He laughed out loud. 'Anaa, come with me to make a snowman.'

'It's not snowing enough to make a snowman; it needs a lot more snow.'

'If it snows like this till tomorrow, will it be enough?'

'More than enough!'

'Will you go with me tomorrow?'

'Yes, Insh'Allah.'

By this time the potatoes were ready. I put them out on two plates and carried them to the dining table with fresh mint chutney.

Mobin salted his potatoes and wolfed them down. Then he got up, went into the kitchen and started rummaging in the cupboards. He returned with two sticks, a carrot and a few large leaves of white and jasmine lettuce. He left again, this time making for his room. He brought back a handkerchief, a hat, two gloves and a plastic bag. When the snow had settled, he would be ready.

The next morning, Mobin and I left the house. There is a large clearing near our apartment block. In the summer it is covered in grass and wildflowers, today it was blanketed in snow. A number of little boys and girls came out of other apartments; some hurled snowballs at each other, others packed the snow into blocks of ice. Mobin looked up and snow fell on his face. He shook it off and said to me, 'It's a wonderful day, isn't it, Anaa?'

When the snowman was done, Mobin placed his hat on its head. All the children surrounded our snowman. Some said it was beautiful, some said this feature or that wasn't done right. Then, from further off, we heard a boy shouting: 'Quick! Run away! They are coming!'

The children looked around and then ran to

hide. Suddenly they'd all gone silent. My eyes fell on two men with long sticks in their hands coming towards us. They approached the snowman. One of them knocked its head off and the other started smashing its body. Mobin wrapped his arms around me and held on tightly. I held his head with both my hands.

The men went on to destroy other snowmen in front of other blocks. Furious, I turned back towards our apartment.

'Now was it easier to build that or destroy it?' I asked Mobin. He replied sadly, 'It was a good day, but they ruined it.'

When we reached our apartment, Mobin cheered up. He felt safe here. He lay down on a mattress but quickly got up again. He said: 'Anaa, do you know why the Taliban broke the snowman?'

'You tell me,' I said.

He reflected, 'They are not scared of the snowman. The snowman is not real, but if they beat a man like that, the poor man would die!'

12

#CapturetheAfghans

12 January–28 February

The writers' realities are increasingly disparate and dispersed: nowhere is it easy, but nowhere in exactly the same way.

Nilofar, Mazar-e-Sharif

In the last few days, the presence of the Taliban in Mazar has doubled, as if to drive everyone away. We cannot live under the shadow of the Taliban.

Parand, Kabul

Uff, I've always attributed the Taliban's anti-social nature to the vigilance of its leaders, who isolated ordinary people from culture and civilisation so they could become more single-minded as soldiers. But watching them in recent days, I am starting to think these soldiers are beyond anti-social and moving towards sadism. They have no purpose but to harass people who have no power and watch them suffer.

Najla, Kabul

I'm waiting on the side of the road for the office van. Snowfall is forecast all day today. I'm the only woman on the road. A taxi driver is sitting in his car waiting for a customer and now another elderly woman has arrived. She directs the driver to the side of the block, where there

are several suitcases on the pavement. She's
definitely going to the airport. My heart wants
to know where she is going and how she got the
visa.

I get into the van with my colleagues. At the
checkpoint, a Taliban soldier knocks on the
window of the passenger seat but my colleague in
front doesn't lower the glass. Maybe he's fallen
asleep: he lives far away and is picked up early.
The Talib pulls open the back door. My other
colleague next to me has make-up on, her lipstick
is red. I'm wearing full hijab, but there are small
flowers on my handkerchief. I'm worried.

There must be questions in the Talib's mind. He
seems surprised for a moment when he looks
into the car, but he doesn't ask questions.
Another soldier demands the driver's licence,
and our frightened driver helps him read what is
written on the faded document. Then the first
Talib smiles and says: 'Don't be upset. Go,
move.' I relax a little. I don't know how long I
can go to the office in fear.

Zainab, Abu Dhabi, UAE

Today I woke to the sound of an explosion and
the scream of an ambulance. For a moment, I
was confused about whether I was in Kabul or
Abu Dhabi. I looked out of the window. The
area was quiet. For a few days now we've been
confined to our rooms, but we could hear an
ambulance far away. I had no idea what
happened until I read the news about Houthi

attacks in Abu Dhabi.* My heart clenched. It is as if wherever we go, war follows! Little by little, I've started to believe the voices in my head: *We will never escape from our destiny.*

Najla

It is still ten in the morning. I have an important meeting today. A foreign representative wants to come to our office with her Afghan colleague. We are concerned about their safety. Our office security is not strong.

The meeting is due to begin at eleven o'clock. Foreigners are very punctual. My colleague makes a call; the foreign woman says they are not allowed to move from their place, and would we mind coming there instead? A few of us get ready to go, then my colleague gets another call. We should not go either. There are security issues. We'll talk in two weeks.

Our office budget is running out.

Zainab

Last night, we heard strange noises around the camp. I couldn't make out the sounds, and every time they got louder, I started shivering. Perhaps

---

*On 17 January 2022, the Houthis, a rebel group (with Iranian support) that partially controls Yemen and is at war with the official government of Yemen (backed by Saudi Arabia and Western governments) initiated a cross-border attack on the United Arab Emirates by launching missiles and drones that set off explosions in fuel trucks near the airport in Abu Dhabi. Three people were killed in the attacks.

it is because of yesterday's attack. Maybe now the military is getting ready. I don't know. Even today you can hear ambulances and there is a strong smell of burning in the area. We looked out of the window, but we couldn't see any fire. Some people started weeping and the children became restless. Then the guards told us to close the windows and stay inside. We could learn nothing more about what was going on.

Nilofar

Zainab jan, you can make a good thriller story out of your experiences. But I hope things get better for you and everyone there.

Nilofar

I can only try to imagine how horrible the situations are in these camps. Thank you for sharing and inspiring me with your writing despite the hard times everyone is going through.

Zainab

Nilofar jan, thank you for reading my writings, sharing your kind thoughts and motivating me to write. I hope you and your beloved family are doing well and living in peace.

Honestly, I try to write in the best way I can, given all my feelings. Sometimes it is very strange to think that we've come to a safe place but it is still a country going through war. Now everything is scary. We get put in quarantine because of the new coronavirus and because of the war situation.

Najla

The door to our office room opens. Salim, the
cleaner, comes in to fill the tank of the heater. In
his hands are a bucket and a jug full of oil. He
trips and oil spills across the floor. The room is
filled with the smell of diesel. Salim apologises
and starts to clean the floor. He breathes heavily.
He says, 'I fell because my thoughts are
elsewhere. For several days, I have received phone
calls from various numbers. They say, "Your
brother was working for the intelligence services,
he should report to the new authorities." They
say that my brother-in-law also served at the
presidential palace. I've blocked all the numbers,
but now I'm getting calls from other numbers. I
don't answer.'

I try to reassure him and start to work, already
thinking about how I will cross the checkpoint
again in the afternoon.

Nilofar

The news of unrest on the border of Ukraine
and Russia worries me. It seems as if the people
of these countries might lose their peace and
security like us. I am worried about the women
and children, the old and young. They cannot
fight. War makes everyone miserable. It disturbs
and displaces everyone. I hope they keep their
peace.

༄

Zainab

I dreamed of the old days.

We were all together in our old house. My sisters
and brothers were planting flowers in our small
garden. My mother and father had gone to a
funeral and stayed there for lunch. I was sitting
in one of the rooms, separating the textbooks
from the storybooks. I found one of my sister's
paintings among the books. I thought of
hanging it on a wall. That was when I heard
shooting outside. The noise of the children
suddenly subsided, and only the sound of
gunfire echoed through the house. I went to the
door, but the yard was full of smoke. I couldn't
see anything through it.

A woman entered through the back gate. I did
not know her. She had a pistol in her hand. She
took my hand and said: 'Come with me, away
from that side. Who else here is with the
Taliban? Let's get them all to safety.' I was afraid
and went with her without saying anything,
leaving my siblings behind.

Once we had left the gates, I tried to call my
parents to tell them what had happened. But I
couldn't. I remembered my little sisters and how
I had left them. After a while I sat on the floor,
heavy with shame. I wanted to go back but I
knew it was too late. As I tried to make my way,
I saw people carrying bodies. They were laid on
the ground, and I searched in tears. One of them

was my sister. I shook her and said, 'Fati!' She was alive. But what had happened to Zahra and our little brother?

I felt ashamed for hours after waking up. I abandoned my family and selfishly ran for my own life. I am a coward!

෪

Atifa, Herat

In August, Atifa's father had just died and at first the fall of the country didn't register in comparison. But the diary kept her connected to other people, as the enormity of what had happened in Afghanistan slowly dawned on her. By now, she was no longer able to work: her organisation, which provided informal education to girls and women, was forced to close its operations.

The latest changes in Afghanistan have been like a tornado, wreaking havoc in everyone's lives – there are only ruins left behind. I feel as if we are dying every day. I don't think about my wishes or hopes like before. I feel as if everyone in this country just tries to survive. It is meaningless to hope or wish, forbidden in fact. My sister took the university entrance exam this year, but she could not go. My friends who had plans became homeless as refugees. One of my brothers went to Iran to find work. My other brother is also thinking of going to Iran as he cannot feed his wife and kids here. All his wishes and hopes have vanished. His only aim now is to earn bread and feed his family.

Marie, Viersen, Germany

Marie has been in Germany for two months. She lives by herself in an apartment three floors up. The building is on a corner, with windows on three sides. Each morning she looks out, at the trees on the hills in one direction, and then the other way, at buses and cars driving down the street. She feels a little purposeless having been used to working hard.

A good thing happened yesterday. I received my residence permit for three years. I now have the right to live, work, study and use all government facilities in Germany. On my way back home, I planned in my mind what I should do to integrate faster and better in this place, the first thing being to learn the language better.

But to start a new life in a new place with new people requires a lot of energy. Sometimes I feel I don't have it. It is never easy to fight alone, without a family, without parents. Some days I squat in a corner of my room and cry. I tell myself, if the Taliban leave the country tomorrow, I will pack my bags and go back to the same ruined place I came from. How many lives can a person start in a lifetime? If only we could bend time as we wish. The night is long and so is my life story. I only hope that at the end of this dark night, one bright morning, my people will wake up with hope again.

These days, I am just so tired of fighting for life.

Zainab

The sky of Abu Dhabi is very different from the sky of Kabul. Here the sky seems so far away, and at night it is coloured red. Some say it's because of the Persian Gulf, some say the desert. There are nights when the red is so vivid it feels magical.

One night it rained so hard it made holes in the sky, as we'd say back home. It really did feel as though the sky had been pierced. Water started collecting everywhere on the ground. If it had rained like that in Afghanistan, it would surely have caused floods. At some point, young people from the camp ran into the storm, laughing and singing wildly. Then the children followed them. The camp workers, sheltering under cover, watched in amazement – were these people drunk or mad?

Elahe, a village near Tehran, Iran

The hashtag #CapturetheAfghans has been trending on social media in Iran. This is not new. Iranian police have been capturing and deporting Afghans for years. I witnessed this horror first when I was a child and playing with friends outside our home, on a street where many Afghans lived. The police would come and pick up all the refugee men they could find and take them to prison. People ran away and hid but the police searched houses one by one. It is hard to escape in Iran unless you don't look at all Afghan. Even students are not safe from this horror. My

friends are routinely taken to the Askarabad
Camp,* and no one listens to them there, even if
they have the right ID.

We run away from one misery only to fall into
another.

*Even today, after spending her whole life in Iran, Elahe's residence
permit carries restrictions. For example, she can only travel
within the city where she lives; to travel further she needs express
permission, and some cities are off limits altogether to Afghans.
The permit itself has to be renewed annually, for a fee.*

Fakhta, near Tehran, Iran

We haven't had a calm day either due to this
#CapturetheAfghans. My husband couldn't go
to work today for fear. And if we are afraid to
go to work, how are we going to feed ourselves?

*Fakhta and her husband have found a place to live outside
Tehran. Her husband continues to pick up daily work on
construction sites.*

Fatima, Semnan, Iran

*Fatima and her parents have been in Semnan, Iran for nearly a
month. Her parents both struggle with their grief and she is their
only support. However, she has a sister nearby who is married,
and was already living in Iran; she can't do much to help Fatima
and their parents, but her visits lift their spirits.*

---

*The Askarabad Camp is a refugee camp in the north-east of Iran. In the
1980s it housed Afghan refugees fleeing the Soviet invasion of Afghanistan;
now it houses Afghans fleeing the Taliban regime.

Now we are in Iran, where women do not wear the full hijab, the internet works fast* and there are many facilities, but we don't have freedom. Refugees in Iran don't have freedom of speech, the authorities do not have good manners with us. We speak the same language, but they don't understand what we say.

They don't want to accept refugees. Our relatives say, 'It is better here; you have to learn not to complain about the little things. At least we can earn three meals a day without fear of the Taliban. You are just a refugee here.' But I was free before and had never been a refugee. Now it turns out the Iranians don't like refugees.

Masoma, Stockholm, Sweden

Today is 31 January 2022. I met everyone from Untold online. I was happy to hear your voices after all these months. My Kabul memories are refreshed. I was so excited to hear Lucy, Negeen, Batool, Najla and Elahe. I was happy and tearful. In just a few months, we've been dispersed to different parts of the world. Many families are in the same situation. We were like a family in Kabul, and now we are apart.

Zainab

Here in the camp, the workers are from many

---

*The messaging platform on which the writers share their diary entries is, however, restricted in Iran, and so to use it the writers need a VPN. The connections are often disrupted.

countries and different backgrounds, as I think
I've mentioned before. They all came here for
work. Perhaps they are lucky to have got that
opportunity. But they work very hard. After the
recent storm, they spent half a day cleaning
standing water from the ground.

They are very kind to the children in the camp.
They treat these children as if they are missing
their own. Now the Afghans have taught them
some Dari phrases like, 'O bacha, o son,' and
'Ana gandagi, look at this mess,' those phrases
have gone viral here. All the Afghans go to
morning prayer together and stand side by side.
It makes me happy. It is as if our own divided
ethnic groups have come together here and
accepted each other.

⁍

Nilofar

Every year at this time of year the Tasadi Bridge
in Mazar would be filled with tree seedlings and
flowerpots for sale. Last year, my colleagues and
I went to the bridge several times to see and buy
plants. We enjoyed seeing greenery in the winter
season, especially when the seedlings were close
to blooming.

But this year, the Tasadi Bridge does not have its
previous prosperity, and no one comes to see the
plants.

Freshta, Dushanbe, Tajikistan

Today it is one year since my mother's death. I haven't felt good since morning. I had a doctor's appointment and tried to spend my day outside to draw this pain out of my chest. I wanted to do this for my baby. I thought if I was upset and cried, it might affect her. But I couldn't dispel the image of my mother from my eyes. I touched the scars on my heart and cried for her – not just for losing her but for every moment of her life. In my mind, I saw a fourteen-year-old girl who was married to someone her father's age, whose first wife had died. I saw a girl who never got to go to school, but had to wash, cook and feed the family. Despite all her suffering, she became a mother in a place without doctors or nurses. She had one boy, and one boy was not enough for Afghan society. Then she had eight girls. Her tenth child was a boy again.

Today I am waiting for my first child's birth. In these nine months, I've known so much pain. But my husband helped me with the housework and did the difficult chores. My mother did all the housework, while giving birth to ten children. And through all this she was trying to have another son.

She never touched a book, but she sent all her daughters to school. She didn't want her daughters to remain illiterate. When there were seminars or gatherings for writers in Kabul, my mum went with us. She could not read or write, but she was there to protect us when it got dark.

Now she is gone. She died from an illness last year. A refugee in another country, I could not attend her funeral. I could not see her one last time and say goodbye to her. I wish I could give her the life that she deserved. I wish that I could have brought her out of Afghanistan and let her breathe fresh air. That I could have released her from the dark prison of tradition and culture. She opened her eyes in that country and closed them there and I feel responsible for that. I wish I could have given her just one day of a better life.

Parand, Kabul

Everywhere I turn, I hit a wall. I want to get a passport. But the passport department is closed. I want to get my birth certificate, but the registry office is not functioning yet. We keep going to the probate court to get a marriage certificate, but the same story repeats itself. These days, all doors close in our faces. What century are we in?

Other governments do everything they can for the rule of law in their societies, but in this country, alas, the opposite is true. Here, we are the Taliban's hostages. It is truly very sad to feel like a prisoner in your own country.

Naeema, Kabul

The war spread fanaticism and violence towards women. And I don't think this situation will change soon. Some families do not allow their daughters to go to school. The girls and women of Afghanistan who live in the villages do not

know the outside world. They only live because
they are alive. They work around the house, and
a moment's break is their only wish. The most
they can hope for is a new dress or headscarf.
These girls and women wait until others decide
they should marry – and call it destiny. There is
a century's distance between village and city life.
We were behind and still went backwards.

Nilofar

Since the winter solstice, a new wave of illegal
migration to Iran has started. Every day, as we get
closer to spring, the fear of civil war grows. My
dreams are dead inside me. I thought it would be
impossible to overrun the republican government,
but it fell. I don't believe in anything any more.
My sister keeps insisting that we should leave the
country, even if it means being smuggled to Iran.
I've always had documents for everything; I'm
afraid of doing anything illegal and without the
right documents. Especially going to Iran. I just
wish we had our passports. Having a passport
feels like having wings. I just hope we don't have
to go to Iran illegally.

*Nilofar and her brother have passports that have expired; their
sister needs her first passport. The struggle to get passports has
become consuming for them, as it has for many people. The issuing of passports stops and starts throughout the year; there are
crowds of people trying to get passports. Nilofar and her siblings
even employ different middlemen who say they can help, and try
to manufacture a medical need when it is said that priority will
be given to patients needing to travel for treatment.*

Freshta

It is the last month of my pregnancy, and I am waiting for the birth of my baby. I have no contractions yet. From what I have read on the internet, contractions start with slow pain that gradually increases. I see some other signs, but I'm not sure whether to alert someone.

The nights are long, and I am restless. I look out of the window but there is no light. The days are better, I can do housework and get on my computer and write. But at night I am so dizzy I can't even write. My body needs sleep, but I can't get any. I went to the doctor and told her about the pain, but she advised me to be patient.

I waited four years to become a mother, but now I am scared. I hide this feeling but day and night I think about how I will give birth to my child. I am not selfish, but I love myself. I am afraid I may have a difficult birth and die. Many women have lost their lives in childbirth, so sometimes I sit and reflect on my life and how it's gone. If these are the last days of my life, I should look carefully at everything around me and spend my time with those I am close to. Nobody knows when their life will end, but I hope I will be alive to hold my daughter in my arms.

Nilofar

It didn't work. We went to so many efforts to get our passports and it didn't work at all. The

passport officials rejected our hospital's letter.
My sister is very upset. I tell myself that, as soon
as she gets her passport, I will send her abroad
in any way possible. I told her, 'Don't worry
about the future, just prepare yourself to face it.'

I believe these days will pass and things will
change, I just hope we have the patience to wait.

Parand, Kunduz

Same here, my dear.

Parand

I had to come to Kunduz Province to renew my
passport. My husband is from Kunduz. Here
too, there are a lot of problems getting
passports. Men, women with babies, and
children of ten or twelve standing outside the
office door. It is freezing cold. Every five or ten
minutes, a Talib pushes the women into the
corner with the butt of his gun. If a woman
steps forward to ask for information, the Talib
pushes her back. More interesting than that is
their process of taking a list of applicants'
names. They decide the order of who will be
seen, based on that list. There are far fewer
women – maybe between eighty and ninety,
standing outside with young children. But they
take the men's applications first, and they
number close to one thousand.

Nilofar

Parand jan, it seems we both have no choice but
to leave by way of an illegal route.

Parand

Yes, I don't see any other option.

Nilofar

In my whole life, this is the first time I fear the coming of spring. I hate winter, I've never liked cold weather, but this year I am reluctant to leave its chill. Because spring brings news of war. Some are predicting the start of a civil war in Afghanistan this spring, and that worries me the most. I hope all the predictions will be proven wrong and everything becomes fine in spring, so no one is forced to flee the country any more.

∽

The next week

Parand

I woke up in a better mood today. I chose my clothes for work, I picked a pink scarf to wear. The idea was to fight against my normal attire, which is all black, from head to toe. Who knew that fighting against darkness would cost me so much? As soon as our office car turned onto a roundabout, the Taliban stopped us. A Talib with long beard and hair gestured to the driver to lower the windows.

'Where to?'

'To the office.'

Then the Talib pointed at me, full of hate. 'Who is she?'

With a jolt of the heart, I returned to the reality this Taliban has created for us. Like a rice field in the wind, I started shaking. The driver was scared too. He said, 'She is our colleague.'

Again, full of spite, in terrible language the Talib addressed the driver, while pointing at me: 'Tell her to dress appropriately. Advise her.'

To free us both from this burden, the driver nodded his head in agreement. As we started moving again, my fear melted and turned into anger. I felt humiliated. What kind of clothes am I supposed to wear? All in black isn't enough? Why is it a sin to wear a colourful scarf? Why are these people against women and what they choose to wear? What further humiliation will we see in the coming days?

Freshta

The Taliban arrested four girls who came out to protest against them, and their situation is unknown. They were arrested because they asked for their fundamental rights: education, work and freedom. That's all they asked: nothing forbidden in law or a sin in any religion.

Last night, I got an email from an unknown sender – a woman, I think. It was sent to more than sixty journalists and said: 'The evacuation process from Afghanistan has started again. We

want to evacuate you from Afghanistan. Please
send us your location and a case number if you
have one.'

I ignored the email because I am already out of
the country, but I felt terrible for the girls in
Afghanistan. Who gave the email addresses of
sixty journalists and civil society activists to this
stranger? What if they get in trouble? Who will
be responsible for that? Since then I've been
worrying about it. Many of us have tried to make
the girls in Kabul aware they should be careful of
corresponding with people who claim they will
evacuate them. I don't know what will happen.

Najla

I feel depressed these days at home. Yesterday
was Friday. After my prayers, I put my prayer
beads made from olive stones in my pocket and
went outside. When I reached the park, the gate
was closed. I was surprised because there were
people inside the park. A man was selling corn
from a trolley. He shouted, '*Madar jan*, dear
mother, the door is closed.' I smiled to thank
him and went to the entrance on the north side.
There a young boy called out to me, 'Madar,
what do you want?' and warned me not to enter
the park.

I asked 'Why?'

'Don't you see there are no women in the park?'
When I looked in, I got goosebumps. I could not
see a single girl or woman anywhere in a park

full of men. The young boy laughed at me and
said: 'There are specific days for ladies. Look at
the timetable on the wall. Can you read?' I did
not answer him. I looked at the wall. There it
was written:

'Sunday, Tuesday and Wednesday are for ladies
and the rest of the days for men. Please follow
the rules strictly. Men and women are not
allowed to be in the park at the same time.'

Two Taliba passed by with their guns and asked
me to go away. I remember the older woman I
met in the park a few weeks ago, the one who
said, 'What if the Taliban closes the park to
women?'

Parand

'*Khala*, Auntie, get in the car . . . Khala, get out
of the car . . . Khala, excuse me . . . Khala, how
many tomatoes do you need? . . . Khala . . .
Khala . . . Khala . . .' Women and girls are all
being called Auntie now by shopkeepers, drivers
and street vendors. It's a form of humiliation.
They used to call older women Khala to remind
them they were no longer young. Now they even
call young girls Khala, to imply they aren't
young or beautiful any more, as if they have
aged and are no longer attractive.

Today, I went to the Ministry of Health for work
purposes. I needed to ask directions from a
Taliban guard. In a tone of pure hatred, he
replied, 'Go that way, Khala, and don't ask too

many questions.' I told myself it was okay, he was just a Talib. He has been made to believe women are mentally deficient. But even inside the information section, I was called Khala. Even educated men are using the term, siding with the Taliban.

Nilofar

I learned that two days ago the Taliban came to our area with two ranger vehicles and took a girl away with them. A few weeks ago, they took a few people from our area who were accused of moral corruption. But the girl they took this time was not a girl who could be painted with an accusation of moral corruption. She simply worked in an office. I am worried the Taliban has started arresting office workers now. This has scared us even more, and my sister is beating the drums again to leave this country.

Freshta

Freshta gave birth to her daughter earlier in the month, and shares her story with the group a fortnight later.

My contractions were increasing. I wasn't sure if this was labour or not, because for a month I've had these pains. But my husband knocked on the neighbours' door. They have a car and they drove us to the hospital at midnight.

The initial assessment showed I still had time. So, that night passed and then another day. Then the doctors decided to put me on a drip to induce labour, because the contractions were not strong enough. After four hours, the doctor came and examined me again. The pain was so intense. It was three in the morning. The doctors were attending me, but my husband was not allowed to be present. I asked them to let him in. I wanted to tell my husband, 'If I die from this pain, please do not take my daughter to Afghanistan.'

I was born during the first dark era of the Taliban, and now precisely the same thing is happening to my daughter. We sent an asylum application to Canada a while ago, and my application is still being processed. In labour, all I could think of was to see my husband and tell him not to go to Afghanistan, not to let our daughter's life be destroyed and please to follow up the asylum application to Canada. She has the right to be free and not to see the faces of terrorists. At 3.30 a.m. I was taken into the operating theatre for a C-section. When the drugs had worn off, I thought about my daughter and asked the nurses to take another message to my husband. I asked them to let him know I was glad our daughter was healthy and I was alive to see her.

Rana, Melbourne, Australia

Freshta jan, thank you for sharing this happy news. So happy your daughter was born healthy. May God bless you both.

Rana was often among the first to respond to good news shared in the group. She says amid so much bad news, she felt encouraged when good things happened to her fellow writers.

Freshta

Thank you, Rana jan.

Parand

Congratulations to you, dear.

Naeema

Congratulations, dear Freshta jan.

Najla

O Freshta jan, bless you. May Almighty Allah
bless you and your daughter with good health
and a beautiful life. Ameen.

Zainab

Congratulations, Freshta jan. I didn't
understand much of what you wrote in Pashto.
But it looks like you have got yourself a little
freshta, an angel, like yourself.

Freshta

Thank you, all, so much.
And yes, I have a daughter now.

Batool, Rome, Italy

May her every step bring you
blessings.

Masoma

Congratulations, Freshta jan. May God look
after her, under the shade of her parents.

Nilofar

Freshta jan, congratulations.

Farangis, San Francisco, USA

Congratulations, Freshta jan.

Nilofar

I want my first child to be a daughter too. What good news!

Marie

Happy new step, Freshta jan.

Freshta

I always dreamed of having a daughter, Nilofar jan. I've got her now.

Thank you all, so much.

ℛ

Two days later

Farangis

My throat felt dry when my mother called me in America and told me to inform my mother-in-law that the Taliban had reached our street in their search operation.* My parents live a few

---

*The fear of being searched by the Taliban has persisted since they took control of the country, area by area. What is known is that they are searching for weapons belonging to the former military, but even those who have

streets away from my in-laws, which means the
Taliban will be at my in-laws' house in a couple
of hours.

Farangis

After saying goodbye, I called my mother back. I
told her to wear the full hijab, black from head
to toe, and put on her chadari too.

---

no weapons are fearful of the searches. They try to anticipate what the
Taliban may object to in their homes and hide documents and money that
may be seized. It might be said that what they fear more amorphously is the
Taliban's tendency to wilfully destroy things they hold dear.

13
House-to-house searches

Early March

There were two of them. They had walked into our house with their shoes on. Now this is the worst sort of disrespect in our culture. Only thieves enter people's homes in shoes and leave dust on the carpets. They both looked at me. For once, the fact that there was no woman with them made me feel calmer. It meant they were not going to search the women's corners or address any questions to us. At last, we remembered to say Salam. You see, we were worried enough we nearly forgot our manners.

Maryam

જી

Najla, Kabul

Nowadays, I am back at work in the office, but I worry about our home. In Kabul, the Taliban are searching houses, and I am not sure when they will come to us. We know they are mainly searching for weapons held by members of the former military, but we never know what else they might object to. These days, until midnight I think about what to hide and where everything is, and what the Taliban may not like. We live in an apartment and all our shelves and cupboards are piled with books and papers. We keep all the old contracts of the places we've worked alongside our ID and passports – we have these things gathered in case life becomes unbearable and they help us to leave the country.

We have heard that the Taliban also search the basements of apartment buildings. We don't know what to do – we are reluctant to set everything on fire and burn our identity. Most of our books are old and irreplaceable. They are from the time when Afghan publishing houses hand-typed their books. I remember when the Taliban came the first time, in 1996, the publishing house that brought out one of my uncle's books came under rocket fire. All the books there were burned, the only three copies of my uncle's book that still exist are the ones we saved at home.

I took a big travel wallet from the cupboard and put into it my cash savings, our passports and ID cards, the copies of our contracts, and the deeds for our apartment that I was given during the Soviet era as a government employee. On the deed is a picture of me when I was young, with no headscarf. I put a few more documents in the wallet and thought I would place it against my body and wrap my big scarf around me when the Taliban came – since they don't speak to women. But then I heard that they have women accompanying them, to search the women in houses. I don't know what to do. Should I keep the documents with me or think of something else?

৪০

As soon as I returned home in the evening, I
noticed a change. The Taliban were standing
outside our building, every one of them holding
a gun. Some wore uniforms, some were in
ordinary clothes walking around the block, and
some were sitting in cars. When I entered our
apartment, I saw all my family looking as
anxious as I felt. It was getting dark, and we
knew they didn't search houses in the evening:
maybe our turn would be early the next morning.
My son Matin asked what we were going to do
with the documents.

I replied, 'Let me think. We will find a way to
hide them.'

'Mor, we are losing time. I could take them now
to my cousin's house if you wish?'

'No, they live far away, and you'll have to take a
taxi. They are also searching cars on the road.
They search anyone carrying anything.'

'So, what shall we do?'

I smiled to see my son so worried and calmed him
down, saying, 'Don't worry, I have made a plan.'

৪০

In the morning, I got ready to leave for the
office. If someone followed me, they may have
observed that I was carrying a heavy handbag.

Even at home, I tried to be strong and not show that I was worried. I dressed in my long black hijab, which covered me from head to toe, wore a black mask and a brown headscarf, and went out. Luckily, the main gate was still open. When the Taliban were conducting a search, they closed all the gates. The whole block was quiet.

When I was coming down the stairs I heard the Taliban soldiers. I did not look towards the sound and carried on as if I didn't hear anyone. I was scared and could feel a heat at my back. What if they called out to me?

I was lucky. I exited the security gates of the block, feeling triumphant that I had made it out. I waited for the staff van to my office. Only when I saw it coming did I look back at our building. Two Taliban were there, one wearing a white turban and the other in a black turban, both in camouflage. The trees stopped me seeing precisely whether or not they were looking at me.

I sighed with relief as the vehicle moved off and I held my handbag on my lap. I told my colleagues the Taliban were searching our home today. I pretended to be cheerful, so my colleagues would not notice my anxiety when we passed checkpoints.

At the office, I received a call from home to update me that at 11 a.m. our apartment had still not been searched. I was anxious. I worried about my daughters and the bag next to me. I did not say to anyone in the office that my handbag was especially significant today.

One of my colleagues called the office security guard outside and asked him where the Taliban were. The guard replied that the Taliban were on the main road in their cars and hadn't begun searching our office quarter yet. My colleagues are young girls who immediately wanted to leave the office while there was time. I said I would stay, and they protested that they couldn't leave me alone. But they were scared, and I told them they should go. They left one by one so no one would see them leave together and realise where they'd come from. I sat in front of my computer but couldn't focus on my work.

From the window, I could see the Taliban going into people's houses. I drew the curtains and hid behind them. The office was dark, and I was sitting in it alone with my handbag full of documents. I wished now I had left the office with the other ladies.

80

After a while, I turned off my computer, grabbed my handbag and left the office. At the gates, I saw the security guards were also terrified. I asked them to let me out, but didn't mention that I was leaving for the day. No taxi or other vehicle was stopping on the road because all travel was suspended during the search. I tried to walk calmly, so no one would suspect I was carrying anything important.

The weather is still cold, but I was sweating as if it was summer. I walked a long distance, until I reached a bus stop. I did not want to take a taxi. I boarded a bus towards the city and got down near a shopping mall. I did not know how to spend my time and I didn't want anyone to notice that and follow me. I went into the mall; I used to come here with my colleagues sometimes to look at the nice clothes. I browsed the shops for a while and checked my mobile.

Time was not passing. I had only been there an hour. I went to the second floor and saw a dress I liked. I asked the shopkeeper how much it was and hoped he wouldn't offer to lower the price. That way I could just walk away. But he immediately suggested a discount. I had to make an excuse about checking other shops. He was annoyed. 'Are you just window shopping?'

I was exhausted. I went to a restaurant and thought I would eat and drink and pass some time there. I did not have the appetite to eat anything, but I asked for a burger. There were some other ladies in the restaurant too. They were talking about the house-to-house searches. I didn't want to listen. I called home and was told the Taliban had just entered our block and would be in our home soon. Again, my whole

body was seized with pain. I started praying in
my heart.

For two more hours I walked the roads, until I
checked my phone and saw a WhatsApp from
my son. It said, 'The search of the whole block is
over, please come home, please.'

Spring

I see swollen branches around my quince tree. The neighbour brings out more red carpets to air on her roof. I see tears in her eyes. Maybe she's remembering last autumn when she sent her young daughters to Iran alone. She sits in a corner and watches a bee hovering over the quince blossoms. At last, spring in my land: blessings will come.

Maryam

14
Nowruz
1–31 March

Seasonal renewal comes, but not without worrying news. In Afghanistan, it is finally Nowruz, the celebration of a new year. On the first day of spring, girls go back to school with high hopes, only to be sent away again. The writers are furious.

Marie, Viersen, Germany

Marie likes Germany. She especially likes that women live for themselves and not only for their children. She got on a bus and found a woman driving it who was covered in tattoos. Marie thought she looked fantastic and told her so. There are three other Afghan families in the same town; the families of former colleagues who were evacuated from Afghanistan at the same time. She didn't know them in Kabul but now they talk and cook together.

The saddest aspect of my days in Europe has been seeing the flag of Ukraine flying in every house, market and shop. I am not at all against this action, to show solidarity with Ukraine. But when I see the Ukraine flag, I ask myself, what did the world do for the people of Afghanistan? Is Ukraine different from a country in the Middle East and Asia? I know the Ukrainians are white, with blue eyes, and they are European. But humanity is humanity.

Nilofar, Mazar-e-Sharif

Racism is rising sharply in Europe too.

Freshta, Dushanbe, Tajikistan

Today I went outside. The town was crowded, there were balloons and it seemed as if the whole city was celebrating. It is 8 March: International Women's Day. In Tajikistan it's a public holiday and also Mother's Day. Women are wearing colourful dresses and make-up, and they look happy.

Cakes and gifts are for sale in the shops. I had an appointment with the hairdresser, but when I entered, the place was packed and there was a long wait. So, I cancelled my haircut and went back home. All the way, I was upset, thinking about how Kabul turned grey with the arrival of the Taliban. They painted over pictures of women on the signs for beauty parlours and beheaded mannequins in shops. I weep every day for the destiny of women in my land. Happy International Women's Day.

Parand, Kabul

Afghan women are celebrating this day despite losing their rights and disappearing from society. We also celebrated at our office, though most of the participants were men. There used to be twenty-three women in my office, but now fewer than ten women come to work. Some of our old colleagues have gone to other countries, but the women who remain revived the atmosphere of

previous years with beautiful words, poems and
gifts. When I returned home, my husband had a
cake, flowers and silver jewellery ready to
celebrate this day with me. I was so happy to see
men who are not affected by the current
circumstances and have not yet forgotten us.

*Parand first met her husband while on a work trip to Kunduz
Province. She was struck by his honesty – the value that means
more to Parand than anything else. They began seeing each other,
but were worried because she is Pashtun and he is Hazara and
marriage between communities is frowned on by many. Parand
couldn't think how to tell her own father, but she did. He was
shocked but after a year her brothers were able to talk him round
to giving his blessing for Parand to marry again. Parand describes
herself as so happy to be married to her husband and so happy
to be part of a new community that she had not known before.*

₧

Fakhta, Tehran, Iran

*It has been three months since Fakhta and her husband arrived in
Iran, newly married. She has managed to find work in a tailoring
shop and her husband still works on construction sites. It is difficult
to find work as an Afghan refugee, but sometimes it is possible, she
says, because employers get away with paying Afghans less.*

Our house contract is coming to an end. The
landlord has asked for an increase in the rent, or
we will need to leave. Since we moved to Iran,
my husband has been working very hard as a
labourer, but we don't have enough of an income
to save anything. We can't even repay the loan

we took to pay the smuggler who brought us over the border from Afghanistan.

When our landlord came to see us, we were having dinner. With his words, we lost our appetites entirely and neither of us ate any more. We decided we had better find a new place. My husband and I sat and wrote down the names of all our relatives living in Iran so, one by one, we could ask them to lend us money. But no one could help. I curse the Taliban a hundred times a day for bringing us such humiliation and hardship.

Finally, my husband had to ask his employer for a loan. His boss agreed on the basis that my husband would continue working for him until his loan was repaid. When we got a call from the real estate agent saying that they had a house for us to rent, we were full of enthusiasm. When we entered their office, we were introduced to a middle-aged Iranian woman, who was the owner of the house. As she was in a hurry, the agent immediately began writing out the contract. I didn't hear what he then asked my husband, but when my husband answered the landlady turned to us. 'Are you Afghan?' We said yes and she promptly addressed the agent. 'Mr Ahmad, I will not rent out my house to the Afghan crowd. I've always been very sensitive about this issue. I prefer to leave my house empty than rent it to Afghans. Please inform me when you find suitable tenants.'

She walked out. I wanted to ask her why she
wouldn't rent her house to Afghans, but I felt I
already knew the answer. The people of this
land prefer animals to Afghans. There is a lot of
hatred, discrimination and ego in this land too,
unfortunately.

Mehrsa, Iowa, USA

*It is seven months since Mehrsa arrived in America. She has
found living in small-town Iowa a challenge: it is quiet, cold and
snowy and feels very white. Her siblings all live together in Iran,
their parents having died some time before the fall of Kabul.*

It's a strange, lonely time in the Midwest. These
nasty crows grate on my nerves as they exchange
news. I remember my mother used to say, if they
sing on your rooftop, it means there is a guest on
the way. I have got no home, so I'm expecting no
guest at my doorstep. What are you saying, you
silly unlucky birds? Are you bringing news of a
third world war or laughing at my desperation?

But then a knock at my door in the university
halls of residence where I live, and there stands a
woman in many layers with a flowery facemask
on. She says in a white voice, 'I was passing your
door and thought I should get you to sign this.'
It's a woman I know, Cassandra, and I see she's
holding a copy of our book, *My Pen Is the Wing
of a Bird*.* My inner voice starts mocking me, *It's
just a small story you have in there, are you really*

My Pen Is the Wing of a Bird is an anthology of translated new fiction by
Afghan women; its contributors are all members of this writers' group.

going to autograph the book?! I've never done this before, but I can try. 'Sure,' I say, 'why not?'

Farangis, San Francisco, USA

I went to a job interview today. It was for a government post in a legal department, exactly what I always wanted and wished for. I was interviewed by a US Army veteran who had fought in Afghanistan. He told me about his experiences in Afghanistan over five years. He said, 'I like Afghan food. I like the Afghan people. The people there are poor but brave and hospitable. A lot of my co-workers are still there. I think about them every single day. Do you have anyone left in Afghanistan?' I could feel a rasping in my throat. Close to tears, I said, 'Yes, all my family. My mother, brother and sisters. All my friends. I cannot sleep at night because I think about them all the time.' He said, 'I respect all Afghans. I feel your pain.' I felt better after talking to him, someone who knew Afghanistan enough to talk to me and understand me. That's the kind of land it is: whoever visits Afghanistan once, loves it forever.

Najla, Kabul

The park Najla goes to is a short walk from her home.

I saw a middle-aged woman at the park who seemed new to me. I believe she is the new female security guard for the park. No matter who comes to the park, she observes them closely, especially the young girls and women.

Most days when I go to the park, I want to get
closer to other people so I can listen to their stories
and learn something. But today I was worried and
had no patience to listen to anyone. I decided to sit
alone. The bench was cold; it was a sunny day but
it is still not warm in Kabul. The temperature must
have been about two degrees. As my grandmother
used to say, at this time of year, the wind wakes the
trees and flowers from their winter sleep.

I took my shoes and socks off and pushed up my
sleeves to get some sunshine. It was about four
o'clock in the afternoon, and the park seemed
friendly and crowded. Now, all the women are
mostly at home in apartment blocks, and they
feel depressed. It's only when the park is open to
women that they can come out for fresh air.

The park never used to get crowded – in the old
days, all these young women and girls were
working or studying at the university. They wore
European clothes then and simple headscarves.
When they came to the park, some would bring
food. Women would spread their picnic blankets
on the grass and sit to drink tea.

By now, the sun's golden rays had warmed my
hands and feet. I felt a bit better.

Nilofar

*Nilofar lives with the same brother and sister with whom she
hopes to leave the country. But while they try every route to get
passports and leave, they must persist with life in the present and
earn a living.*

Today was the last day of the year, and we moved house. I liked the previous house. We were close to the main road, which meant it was easily accessible. It also had a yard. But it was too far from the city and sometimes my brother has to come home very late at night, so we worried.

At first, I was sad to move. But then I thought to myself, all the time that we lived in that house, we faced problem after problem. While we were there, the pandemic came and then the fall of the country. I comforted myself that a change was necessary.

Nilofar

It didn't feel like Nowruz. The city felt sad and exhausted. Only a few of my classmates said, 'Nowruz mubarak, Happy New Year,' to one another. The Taliban has declared Nowruz a Magian tradition.* After the exam, my friends and I went to Rawze-e-Sharif.† While Monday is designated for women, there were a lot of men today. They didn't allow women to enter, so we ended up going to a friend's home. The five of

---

*Nowruz originated as a Zoroastrian celebration, therefore associated with ancient Persia; the magi were Zoroastrian priests. The Taliban dismissal of the festival implies more simply that it is non-Islamic, not aligning with their strict interpretation of Islam.

†Rawze-e-Sharif is a mosque in Mazar-e-Sharif, Afghanistan. Shia devotees believe the mosque contains the tomb of Ali, whom they consider the first rightful successor to the Prophet Mohammed. Many Afghan Shias make an annual pilgrimage to the site to celebrate Nowruz. It is sometimes called the blue mosque of Mazar-e-Sharif.

us in our group of friends have shared beliefs and similar thoughts about so many things. We celebrated a New Year's day in the best spirit. As they say, if the new year is going to be good, you will know by its spring. Let's see how our year is going to be.

Nilofar

I am no longer sad that my hair has turned grey. My friend, who has just turned twenty, told me she has three strands of grey hair. When she is thirty-three, her hair will probably all be white. To be honest, I think it's the events in the country that have turned our hair grey.

∞

Rana, Melbourne, Australia

I talked with my cousin on the phone and asked if his sister Jamila had gone to school today. He said the Taliban announced that, until further notice, the schools are closed. Then I saw the texts from my old colleagues. They shared the news from the education ministry that schools remain closed for girls in Years 7–12.

God knows I was furious. When I used to be a teacher in Kabul, I often asked my students what they wanted to be in the future. I always told them to have a purpose in life, because without a purpose you are colourless. They said they wanted to be doctors, teachers, engineers,

judges. One student said she wanted to lead the
country as president.

*Rana hears this news on the phone from Australia. She loved her
job as a teacher in Kabul: 'When I was little I would teach my
dolls!' she explains. She has been in Melbourne for three months
at this point, going to English classes with her mother and other
older Afghan women, some of whom are going to 'school' for
the first time in their lives.*

Freshta

My husband's little sister cannot go to school again!
I had a video call with her on Nowruz. She was not
wearing new clothes. I asked her, 'Why aren't you
dressed up, Shabnam?' She said, 'Because I bought a
new school uniform for when my school starts on
the 22nd.' She seemed very happy and excited: she
could go without new clothes for Nowruz, but she
needed a new school uniform. She had bought a
uniform that would cover her fully when she
returned for Year 12. She said it was better to be
fully covered than be told off at school.

Yesterday, Shabnam wore her modest Islamic
hijab but was not allowed to enter the school.
The school gates are closed to her. She is
denounced for being a girl. In what state must
she have returned home? I tried to reach her on
the phone all day. We Afghans can take nothing
for granted.

Naeema, Kabul

I also went to school with much hope and
determination. I was sure that after seven

months the girls would be very happy returning
to school, and I wanted to be there to see it.

All the students were gathered in the school
assembly area, and the loud noise of girls talking
was so pleasing. After such a long time, everyone
seemed cheerful and motivated.

But not for long. We heard rumours that schools
might close, but we did not want to believe it.
We sent the students to their classes, and I took
a lesson with Year 9. All the students were sitting
quietly and looking at me. I tried my best to act
normal, but the silence of my students was very
upsetting. I teased them: 'I have never seen you
all so quiet, what happened? Why aren't you
making a noise so I can tell you to be quiet?'

The girls seemed to lack energy, they just smiled.
At this moment, the classroom door opened. A
clerk from the office said that all the students
must come to the assembly point because there
was important news to be shared. It seemed as if
everyone already knew what it was. Yes, the
information was to tell the students to go home:
girls above Year 6 would be informed later when
they could return to school.

I saw the girls all looking down, upset. Some
teachers said, 'Let's protest and take all the
students too.' But it was dangerous. The
girls walked out tearfully, and many cursed
the Taliban. As teachers we decided we could
not let this rest but must slowly begin

demanding for schools to be reopened for
the older girls.

Parand, Kabul

News headlines on Afghanistan media these
days:

> The Taliban has closed secondary schools to
> girls
> The Taliban stopped ten women flying
> unaccompanied
> The Taliban beat several women who did
> not observe hijab regulations
> The Taliban has set aside special days for
> women to use parks and recreation areas

It seems like the women have provided the best
ground for the Taliban's internal political
cooperation. They keep their members together
through this shared purpose: the oppression of
women. I wonder, could the Taliban retain
power if there were no women?

Freshta

I feel very guilty. Guilty about the girls of my
country who had to return home, shut out of
school. I am sorry that you are shut out of school.
Maybe some of you will ask me: *Where were you
when the schools closed, what have you done for us?*

I'll have to reply to you, 'I was a refugee in a
strange land. I saw the news on TV and could
not hold back my tears. I cried hard for you.'
Your reply will be: *We also wept, we screamed,*

*we protested, and no one was there to hear us.
You were a news reporter once, we want to ask
whether you raised our voice to the international
community.* You will demand: *Why didn't you
do something for us?*

Yes, you are right I haven't done anything for you,
and the international community that I knew has
forgotten about Afghans. They think Afghan
women are worthless. They just play whatever
game they like to play with Afghan women. The
international community once came up with the
United Nations 1325 clause,* defending gender
equality; Afghan women worked hard to establish
legislation on child marriage, women's rights,
prohibition of polygamy, education and divorce.
They wanted not to be second-class citizens.
What did the foreigners do? They left halfway,
while Afghan women were making laws to end
the gender gap and bring gender equality. No one
heeded our tears, our hard work. The universe
could hear us, but those in power did not want to
listen. It was as if they had blocked their ears with
cotton wool. We say, 'Only that land is burning,
where the fire is thrown.'

∞

---

*UN Resolution 1325 was a landmark resolution adopted unanimously by
the United Nations Security Council in 2000. It addresses the impact of
armed conflict on women and emphasises the need for the participation
of women in all peace and security efforts of the UN.

Parand

I spent the first days of Nowruz in nature. It was a lot of fun. I feel as if the burden of my tired soul has been reduced.

We had a long car ride. Luckily, no one talked. Alongside the wide road, I could see spring colours beaming. I looked out: the plains and valleys of my country are truly beautiful. The snow was melting on the mountains and green hills could be seen far off. There were apple trees in blossom everywhere. Although I love winter, and I missed the footprints of wolves and foxes that come down from the mountains, spring is also good.

Fatima, Semnan, Iran

It's been three and a half months since depression took over my whole being. I'm looking for a job in Iran, but to get an administrative job I need to have a residence card. Even small shops ask for a work permit. Finally, my neighbour's wife, who felt sorry for me, took me to a restaurant. They said they would give me a dishwashing job and the task of cleaning the toilets. It was better to do something than nothing. The neighbour's wife advised me not to mention that I was Afghan. The boss was very happy with my work. It did not pay much, but it was a good start. However, the next day, I couldn't bear the thought of hiding my identity from my employer. So, I said, 'Sorry but I need to discuss an issue with you. I

am Afghan.' He said, abruptly, 'I am sorry, but
we cannot give jobs to Afghans unless you have a
work permit.'

I felt so bad for being Afghan. Why are we even
here? Neither can we have a place on earth, nor
can our hands reach the sky.

Fatima

This morning, I received an email related to
helping Ukraine.

I really sympathise with the people of Ukraine,
Because I know how war is,
How becoming a refugee feels,
How it feels to leave family and loved ones
    behind,
How the world seems to support you, but in the
    end,
You are all alone,
You are left by yourself,
You become a joke.

But I also know these days pass. I hope that war
gets eliminated from the face of this world.

> ## Najla
> You say it beautifully, Fatima jan, and I agree
> with you.

15
Ramadan

1–30 April

In a fractured holy month, the writers reflect on their surround-ings. In Afghanistan, life is constricted further, in Iran being Afghan itself is a problem. Among Afghans living in a refugee camp in Abu Dhabi, the norms of home alter subtly. Attacks in Afghanistan cause distress for all and, exasperated with the Taliban version of religion, the writers turn to their own prayers.

Nilofar, Mazar-e-Sharif

The cheapest ice cream used only to cost five Afghani, and poorer kids could afford to buy themselves those sticks. With the arrival of spring, children happily took their five Afghani coins in hand but were disappointed to find there was no ice cream under ten Afghani now. So, unable to buy anything, the children just follow the ice cream seller as he rides around on his bicycle-trolley. Even the ice cream bazaar is cold and unexciting this year.

Nilofar

Nilofar has found a new job teaching in a private kindergarten.

Everyone is shocked at the news that a midwife in Ali Chopan* was killed by the Taliban for

---

*A 23-year-old midwife was tortured and murdered by the Taliban on her way home from working at the Ali Chopan Clinic in Mazar-e-Sharif. The Taliban accused her of travelling in public with a man who was not her

238

working without a mahram. There is renewed fear and restlessness in everyone. Where to find a mahram, so you can take him everywhere with you at every moment? The tortures that this girl endured make your hair stand on end. I've found a good job, but in this current situation it is better to give up on the idea of working. I don't want to get into such trouble.

I only wish this was all a nightmare.

Nilofar

I despise all this preaching about prayer and fasting. I wish they would promote humanity instead. How do they expect people to love the idea of paradise when they've made the world hell for us? When their world is like this, what can we expect from their heaven? In fact, their idea of heaven is more terrifying.

Nilofar

The Taliban has ordered that after 8 p.m. all shops and other outlets should shut down and everyone should go to *Tarawih*, prayer. I don't know how they interpret this sentence in the Quran: 'Let there be no compulsion in religion.'

Zainab, Abu Dhabi, UAE

There are all kinds of Afghans here in the camp in Abu Dhabi, among them some good and distinguished men. And then there are men like

---

husband or any other relative. She had got into a car with a male colleague who offered to drive her and her sister's baby home.

hungry wolves, here to ambush girls and women. In this way, the camp is like a small Afghanistan. Indeed, it could be worse because there are many more single men than single women – I would say about one hundred to ten – and they have no occupation. The situation could easily be like Kot-e-Sangi. But this place is different from Afghanistan because its structure and governance are different.

To put it simply, as a woman, I can walk throughout the night without worrying that a man will assault me or act inappropriately. Sometimes my scarf falls from my head, but I don't worry about it. It's usually quiet here. Sometimes only the guards are at their post, and they don't even glance at me, with or without a headscarf. I walk freely in the middle of the night with Sarah, the friend I made while waiting to fly from Mazar. We laugh, run and joke together during our walks, without any fear or worry.

Last night something happened that I have never experienced in Kabul. We took a walk outside after breaking fast. We found a bench not far from the security post. Other people were walking too. There were men who walked past us. A few of them stared at us, and then Sarah started making fun of them, which made me laugh too. We couldn't control our laughter. One of the men heard us and turned back with unspoken anger in his face. His face had turned red. We carried on laughing. Every

time the man took a step away from us, he
turned his head and looked at us. I realised
our situations had been reversed. I was the one
laughing here – it was like an act of revenge
for all the teasing and pranks I endured from
men in Kabul.

Nilofar

*Nilofar was thirteen when she and her siblings returned to live in
Afghanistan, their parents having died some years previously,
while the family lived in exile in Iran. Her first conscious
memories of Afghanistan are from that time. Afghanistan was
not as developed as Iran, she says, but for the first time she lived
in her own country, and that felt very good.*

We moved back to the area we first lived in when
we returned to Afghanistan twenty years ago.
The republican government had just been
established when we returned from Iran. By the
end of the republican era, property here was so
expensive that people like us could no longer
afford to live in the area. But with the fall of the
government and the exodus of many rich people,
rents have gone down again. Of course, the area
is less bustling than it used to be.

When I walk along the streets, I remember those
early days when many refugees returned to the
country. At that time, due to low income,
people, including us, made their own bricks so
they could build a house for themselves. How
quickly a town can grow from zero to one
hundred and then back to nothing. It took
twenty years for people to prosper and now the

tall buildings here are empty once again, because
their owners have gone abroad.

Those twenty years were full of hope. Despite all
the hardships, we still had hopes for our lives.
Now we think more about leaving than staying.
It is a bitter truth. Our twenty years in
Afghanistan are now multiplied by zero.

Zainab

Two types of men live here. There are those who
used to be advisers, viziers and ministers in
government offices. Now they are useless, like
bicycles with a puncture. They roam around
uselessly trying to lure young women with their
names and titles. Then there is the group,
unknown, with a lowly title, who are the most
efficient and useful to society here. The
naanwa-ha, the bread-makers.

Recently, the Arabs have employed Afghan
bakers to work with them. Now they can earn a
little money to send to their families. I think that
baking bread is a very difficult task in this hot
land. They sit next to a hellish oven for hours. A
few nights ago, one man fainted and they took
him to a hospital. Unlike our fleeing president,
this young baker kept doing his job till the very
last moment.

To be honest, the bread is not as tasty as the
bread in Kabul, even though it looks like it. I
don't want to complain, and I know that
preparing several thousand loaves of bread a day

is a difficult task. Also, the bread that the Arabs used to give us tasted like dough and not bread. They either do not bake the bread well enough or they add a lot of dried yeast. I often think of warm Afghan bread with a cup of sweet tea on the side. I cannot tell if it was the magic of the baker or the wheat or the soil that gave life to the bread, but I know that there is nothing more delicious than Afghan bread. Sometimes all I want for myself is warm Afghan bread.

Nilofar

Yesterday, one of my Year 1 students, Mariam, entered the school wearing a big white shawl-scarf. Unlike me, who still does not know how to wear a shawl-scarf properly, she had learned from her mother how to wrap the big shawl neatly around her head and fasten it with a needle.

I was impressed by Mariam wearing a shawl with such skill, but I felt deeply sad. Why would a seven-year-old girl wear such a big shawl? Why should she wear one at all?

Fatima, Semnan, Iran

The saying goes:
> 'The blacksmith sinned in Balkh,
> The coppersmith got beheaded in Shoshtar.'

Such is the situation here these days. A person killed two religious scholars and now, all over Iran, Afghans are being harassed, ill-treated and forced to leave Iran. It is not even known whether the killer was Afghan, but they say he was and now Afghans must take the blame.

Where can we go next?

Fakhta, Tehran, Iran

All these events have become an excuse for the government and people of Iran to rise again against us Afghans. The government arrests Afghans from their doorsteps or the bakery queue, without any further inquiry, sending them to a camp from which they are sent back to Afghanistan. Workplaces are no longer safe either. These days, the situation has deteriorated so far that none of us Afghans dare to go to our workplaces, whether they are construction sites, agricultural fields or greenhouses. In some parts of Iran, people have even started demonstrations to demand the unconditional departure of Afghan nationals.

I told my husband to talk with his employer and see if he could stay home for a few days until the situation gets better. But his boss did not accept that, saying the situation had nothing to do with him. He reminded my husband of the money we had borrowed. These days, from the moment he leaves for work until he is back, I pray. That is my only source of hope.

Najla, Kabul

Najla is one of the longest-standing residents of her apartment block. The apartments in her building have emptied and refilled three times over she says, as people have moved away and gone abroad. So, she doesn't know her neighbours well despite having lived there so long.

Today I entered the park through the middle gate and slowly walked to a bench. A woman was sitting opposite, and we greeted each other.

The weather in Kabul is still cold. I wrapped my scarf around my neck. There are now rays of warming sunshine to touch our skin and a breeze that rustles the trees. In the shade it is still cold, but the snow has disappeared, and you can see the soil.

The woman had a brown handbag on her lap. It looked packed full. She held it tightly and moved a little towards me. I asked her, 'Do you live in this area?'

She pointed to a block of flats. 'Yes, I live there. I have two other houses as well. One is in the city, and one is in Khair Khana. But I cannot handle the gardening, I prefer to live in a flat.'

She went on.

'I had a good life with my husband. He loved me, and we used to have a good understanding.'

'Where is he now?'

She sighed. 'He passed away five years ago due to a health condition, may his soul rest in peace.'

'Ameen.'

'*Khuda ra shokor*, thank God, I have five children, three boys and two girls.'

'Are all of them married?'

'Thanks be to God, it is a blessing they are all settled.'

She told me that three of her children lived in foreign countries and the other two were on US evacuation lists and might leave soon. I asked if she would also be leaving.

'My elder daughter is very kind. She wants me to go to her in America. I have all the paperwork done. I am waiting for my interview.'

'Are you happy to leave?'

'To be honest with you, I am not happy. When my daughter tells me stories of America it sounds like everyone is into his or her own life. It is not the same as here where relatives will come to ask about you. My daughter says even the parks are empty and the birds rarely fly. Everyone is lonely. How can I be happy in such a desolate place?'

'Did you ask her not to tire herself with all your paperwork if you are in two minds?'

'No, I haven't said that to her yet. I am waiting. If I get the visa, I will decide whether to go or stay.'

She turned to me, worried. 'Is this appropriate? Will it affect her residency there?'

'I don't know how it works.'

She told me she'd gone to the market to buy two headscarves for her daughter in America to wear during Ramadan.

'She is praying and fasting, but when she goes out of the house, she doesn't wear a scarf. She says in America, people do not wear a headscarf and those who wear one are not welcomed. I am scared that my life will be in danger if I go about wearing my headscarf. What shall I do? As the proverb goes, "The snakes haven't bitten me yet."'

Zainab

I opened the post today and found our book in it: *My Pen Is the Wing of a Bird*. I held it in my hands and suddenly felt all that I had lost. Before I knew it, tears welled up in my eyes.

Zainab has been writing daily in the refugee camp in Abu Dhabi and from here she sends dispatches to the group. She feels that the experiences she has lived through should be documented, and she is writing them to be read.

Nilofar

I've found hope in life again. Perhaps it's best to get used to the new situation. We went to purchase new mattress covers. My sister kept asking, 'What if we are forced to leave the

country?' I replied, 'We will take them with us.'
As soon as I get a better job with a good salary,
I'd very much like to buy sofas. I've decided to
stay as happy as I can. I will try to have a good
and restful life. I'm happy that slowly I am
fighting my depression.

Masoma, Stockholm, Sweden
Nilofar jan, that's so good to hear. Well done.

I haven't moved from my wheelchair in months. Little feathers are falling around my head. Are these butterflies or quince blossom leaving the tree?

Maryam

Nilofar

Early mornings when I see children going to school, I am very upset. Even little girls must wear a big tied-up shawl around their heads because the Taliban has ordered it. I abhor the Taliban's approach, constantly imprisoning women. The kind of coercion that the Taliban inflicts on people will only make them hate Islam.

God knows what goes on in the minds of these little girls. They are full of hope for life and growth, but they are imprisoned by a new rule every single day.

Fatima

When Fatima entered Iran overland with her parents, in December, they had visas to enter, but these have now expired.

I extended my Iranian visa twice before. This time, they say we must return to our own country to extend our visas. In the meantime, everyone back home keeps calling to say how the Taliban has killed this person or how another person has disappeared. I'm very afraid. My father is still mourning my brother and our displacement. My daily job now is taking him to the doctor. My parents cannot remember everything. I am all alone.

The day before yesterday, I went to the bank. I chose to speak in English. Out of nowhere, an older man standing behind me said, 'You've come to our country, and now you use a foreign language.' He told me to get out of his way. The guard came over only to defend the old man.

I am so lost. Today our visas expired. Now, I am an illegal immigrant. Before this, I had a visa and a thousand problems. Now it is worse.

Batool, Rome, Italy

Fatima jan, don't worry. I hope that this misery ends soon. My whole family is in Iran without a visa. They have made a point not to worry about it. They go to work – what else can they do? They have to survive.

Fatima

Batool jan, thank you. To be honest, the whole world feels like a burden on me. I say there are people of the same language all around us, but not people of the same heart.

Batool

I was about to finish my PhD and my student visa had nearly expired. The consulate told me that I could only stay with a student visa and advised me to return to Afghanistan.

Eventually, I told myself, to hell with legal
status, I will find another hole on earth to be
safe. Then I moved and moved. I am exhausted
but I must persevere and stay alive.

Fatima

I was getting ready to write my dissertation when
we had to leave. My question to God is why we
Afghans are always homeless. I feel like I don't
have a country. I lost my brother for our freedom
– that I and other daughters of Afghanistan
should be educated – and now I am all alone.

Batool

May he rest in peace, dear.

Nilofar

Fatima jan, please do not come back here. If you
come back, you will live in fear. Stay there. Does
the Iranian government deport women too?

Even if you have to come back, don't come back.
Or, if you must, choose a new home, like Mazar.
No one would know you here.

Fatima

I don't know yet. Thank you, Nilofar jan.

৪৩

Zainab

When you return to your senses, you realise you
are imprisoned. Your chains are invisible. That's

when small sufferings start to feel unbearable. Then the pain becomes excruciating and lasts longer. Sometimes it can be a simple thing: a change in what you eat can bring on the pain. You cannot bear the taste of half-cooked onions, but it fills your mouth. You wish to taste cardamom in tea and sweet porridge; instead, it gets stuck between your teeth when you're chewing your rice and korma. It takes away your appetite. Your body craves the eggs you used to have for breakfast – so long since you had one. But you must eat whatever you're given, reluctantly, out of hunger. Maybe you used to see your parents every week. You could be reassured they were doing well and remain calm until the next visit. Now you crave their warm hugs and talks. You come back to yourself and find yourself so far from them. In the camp, you see your neighbour's wife on her phone, leaning her back against the shared wall, tears rolling down her face. You realise she is talking to her mother. You hear there have been explosions and attacks, and your heart burns for your family, but you cannot do anything.

There will be times when you miss your friends a lot, there are things only they would understand. You go silent for a while. You prefer to sit on the stairs at midnight and cry. For a prisoner, the most luxurious prison is still a prison, nothing has any colour or smell there. Nothing moves your heart. For a prisoner, freedom is everything.

Marie, Viersen, Germany

I'm tired of this God that is with the
    Taliban.
The God that doesn't hear the voice of a
    hardworking father,
Or the mother who sits with her tears in the
    heat of the oven.
I'm tired of this God who sits and silently
    watches this show.

I'm tired of all gods because none of them
    listens to our prayers.
We've prayed and cried our eyes out
    everywhere:
In markets, in the maternity hospitals, in
    Kart-e-Sakhi, in Kowsar Danesh, in
    Sayed-ul-Shuhada, in Herat, in Bamyan,
    in Mazar.
And now in Abdul Rahim Shahid High
    School.*
I'm tired of this God who is with the
    Taliban.

Parand, Kabul

Today there was another attack on a tuition
centre for young girls and boys. After reading the

---

*On 19 April 2022, two bomb blasts went off at the entrance of Abdul
Rahim Shahid High School for boys in Dasht-e-Barchi, Kabul. At least six
people, including children, were killed and more than twenty wounded.
The attack was thought to be carried out by IS-K, who had claimed responsibility for similar attacks on the same day. A nearby tuition centre was also
hit in a grenade attack.

news feed on Facebook, I felt as if my heartbeat had stopped. I was very worried about my husband's nieces. I called their mother and she told me they didn't go to school today. But I keep thinking about the innocent children who were killed in a place where they gathered to learn.

Nilofar

What, there has been another attack?

I feel you, Parand jan. Every time, it is civilians who are the victims.

Parand

Yes, the victims are students, six to twelve years of age. Their crime is to be Hazara.

Nilofar

Exactly.

Nilofar

Hazaras have been killed for years and no one is there to support them. But the Hazaras are like phoenixes. We rise from the ashes.

Nilofar

I dreamed last night that I had the Afghan flag in my hand while I was riding my bicycle. I was going to go to a picnic. I hope my dream comes true.

Sadaf, Kabul

Sadaf still lives in the same central Kabul neighbourhood she grew up in, where her group of eleven friends used to plan and coordinate their Eid outfits every year.

255

When we were children, we looked forward to special days. Especially when Ramadan was over, when the bazaar was full of colourful clothes and fabrics, and the whole city was crowded and full of life. We were so excited that we counted the days on the calendar. And on the eve of Eid, we put henna on our hands. We laughed and stayed up late, preparing for Eid. Now, we have reached a point where Eid does not mean anything to us any more. We only know that Ramadan is over, and a day is coming.

ℬ

Later the same week

Nilofar

There have been two more attacks in Hazara areas. A lot of panic has spread among the Hazaras. Eid has turned into mourning. If the situation continues this way, the flood of migrations will intensify. We were trying to get used to this new situation, but it is impossible. It is terrifying to worry about losing loved ones.

Nilofar

Before the start of the holidays, I was hopeful that all my students would return to class. But after the explosions in Mazar, only fourteen students came. I am sure some of them will leave the country soon. But I hope the remaining few will keep coming.

Why do they say that Afghanistan has the world's
saddest people? Why don't they say that
Afghanistan has the world's most hopeful people?

Nilofar

It is past midnight, and I still cannot sleep. I am
worried. I keep thinking about yesterday's
explosion. I am very anxious about the future
and what is going to happen. I try my best not to
think about anything like this, but my mind does
it without my permission.

Nilofar

The second explosion was in the area where we
used to live. I am worried whether I know
anyone who was killed or injured in the
explosion. I hope everyone is okay. I see on
Facebook that the hospitals are asking for blood
donations. It seems like the number of injured is
much higher than reported on the news.

Sadaf

Every year at this time, people bring home
the bodies of their loved ones rather than
new clothes. Some families have two or three
dead bodies. Instead of sharing sweets for
Eid, or wearing new clothes, they grieve.
Today there was an explosion in the Darul-
Aman Mosque* among people who were

---

*A suicide bomb exploded in a mosque in the Darul-Aman area of Kabul
as a congregation gathered for Friday prayers on the last day of Ramadan.
IS-K claimed responsibility for the attack, which was one of the deadliest

praying. Unofficial reports say ninety people were killed, but the Taliban officials say six people are dead and ten are injured. I worry about my land. I don't even want to write any more. I want to sit silently and watch what is going to happen to us.

Sadaf

The government announced that tomorrow is Eid-ul-Fitr.* The sky is colourful from the fireworks. You can hear gunfire mixed with fireworks in Kabul – it sounds the same as it did on 15 August last year. But you can't complain about the sound of shooting and fireworks. This is how people celebrate their happiness – they put their fingers to a gun and shoot.

Farangis, San Francisco, USA

Eid means the arrival of joy and happiness for all Muslims around the world, but it seems that Afghanistan is not on the list.

Let's hold each other's hands and pray.

O Khuda, grant patience to those who have lost their relatives.
O Khuda, grant recovery and healing to those who are sick.
O Khuda, those who are suffering from

Kabul had seen since the withdrawal of US troops, with a death toll of more than 70 civilians.
*Eid-ul-Fitr is the 'festival of breaking the fast'. It marks the end of Ramadan, the Islamic holy month of fasting.

unemployment and poverty, bless them with a
little sustenance.
O Khuda, those who are far from loved ones,
unite them, so their longing ends.
O Khuda, those who are living in camps,
nowhere, help them find a home.
O Khuda, bring peace and security to
Afghanistan.
O God, whoever is suffering from pain, heal
them, whoever has a dream, help to make it
possible.
Ameen.

Nilofar

Ameen.

16
Eid arrives
1–31 May

Najla, Kabul
Salam, dokhtara. I wish you a happy Eid, my
friends. I wish you all happy and blissful days.
Stay safe.

> **Parand, Kabul**
> Najla jan, Eid Mubarak to you too, my dear.

Fatima, Semnan, Iran
Salam, everyone. Happy Eid to you all.

> **Naeema, Kabul**
> Eid Mubarak to us all.

Nilofar, Mazar-e-Sharif
Happy Eid to you all.

> **Zainab, Abu Dhabi, UAE**
> Najla jan, Eid Mubarak to you too, and to all
> the lovely ladies.

Najla
Thank you, Zainab jan. May God ease your pain
of displacement and the pain of all those
suffering. I've been following your journey
through your beautiful journal. All the best.

Zainab

Thank you, dear. This means the world to me.

ℬ

Zainab

All over the world, they require official documents and IDs, don't they?

Today, we had to line up in the hot sun, identity documents in hand, to get toilet paper. I nearly cried from the humiliation. On a large sheet of paper, outside the camp office, they had written that it was necessary to present the ID cards or passports of all family members. It seems a waste of resources – the sheer number of staff allocated to this job – to register each person's identity to hand over toilet paper and sanitary napkins. They had Ugandan guards right outside the office to keep people in order. At times, the staff would emerge and throw out a few words in Arabic. You'd think something very important was going on inside.

I said to Sarah, my friend who used to be a professor at Kabul University, 'Did you ever imagine a situation like this?' She replied: 'This is what it means to become a refugee. You must turn your heart to stone so that you can endure anything that comes your way. This is just the beginning.'

Nilofar

This shall pass, Zainab jan.

Zainab

I wish it would pass, for it seems like a vicious cycle that repeats itself.

Sadaf, Kabul

Sometimes human beings are so hurt that while they pray, they do not wish for happiness. They want peace of mind and a few hours of sleep.

Sadaf

Salam, all. Eid Mubarak to you, and I pray to Allah that you will have prosperous Eid days.

Farangis, San Francisco, USA

Happy Eid to all of you, my dears. May God make this Eid full of joy, blessing, prosperity and happiness, and ease the problems of the sorrowful people of Afghanistan.

Maryam, Kabul

Salam to everyone, Eid Mubarak to you all.

Marie, Viersen, Germany

Eid Mubarak, dear friends in this group.

ॐ

Nilofar

For the first time after these chaotic changes, we went to the park to celebrate Sizdah Badar, the

thirteenth day of spring, by stepping on new
green grass. They had put a curtain up in the
middle of the park, separating men from women.
No more the old joyous noise and laughter.
That's why every ride in the park had been
discounted. We didn't take any of the rides. We
walked for a bit with our bare feet on the grass.
But the air felt constraining. Around 8 p.m., when
we were preparing to leave, it felt as if ghosts had
moved in to the deserted park. I said it out loud
and my brother replied, 'Not ghosts, it's the
Taliban.'

We are getting close to a full year of this
collapse, and news of war and poverty has us
very worried. Our only prayer is that there won't
be another war. I hope you all pray with us.

Zainab

Tonight a young mother died. She lived on my
floor and about a month ago she went into a
coma. Before that, she was hospitalised several
times due to severe depression. I had seen her in
Mazar, I spent a night there in the same room as
her and her daughters. She looked happy then,
as if her daughters were her life and now she
was carrying them to a safer place. But in the
camp, she rarely came out of her room. It
seemed as if the time of quarantine broke her
soul. I am sure her soul is still restless about
leaving her children behind, and that's why
everyone can sense a strange heavy atmosphere
here tonight.

Nilofar

This is very upsetting. Poor soul, she must
have suffered so much. Please, Zainab jan,
take care of yourself and don't worry about
anything. Be strong, and everything will be
fine. Soon, hopefully, you will find a place to
settle down.

> **Zainab**
>
> Nilofar jan, thank you.

Nilofar

Zainab jan, do they not allow you to go to
markets and into the city? If they do, please go
and roam around and find people to talk to.
Perhaps it is a good chance to learn about the
people there and their culture.

> **Zainab**
>
> Nilofar jan, no, we are not allowed to leave the
> camp, and the camp is somewhere far away from
> the city. This is the place they quarantined
> Covid-19 patients before it was turned into a
> camp for Afghan evacuees.

Parand

The pressure on people is increasing every day. To
cover their inadequacy, the Taliban state imposes
ever stricter laws on women. The recent decree on
hijab* is ridiculous. They've said that if a woman

---

*On 7 May 2022, the Taliban's Ministry for the Propagation of Virtue and
Prevention of Vice decreed women must cover their faces in public.

doesn't observe their full dress code they will give
her a warning. If it happens again, they will
punish her. The third time, they will imprison her.

I'm guessing that since this command requires
many steps, they may have to assign a Talib to
watch and follow each girl and woman. A
Taliban approach to governance.

Naeema

Women should not go to offices.
Girls' schools must remain closed.
Women should go to parks only on certain days,
Women cannot travel without a male
  companion,
Offices should be segregated into male and
  female sections.

And this continues for eight months. Every
moment, you feel condemned.

Nilofar

We are inside Afghanistan, and we cannot take
risks and show our opposition to the new law.
Interestingly, those outside Afghanistan do not
make any noise either. It feels as if everyone is
satisfied with the Taliban orders. But we women
feel angry and full of hatred. Death to this
government.

Although the Taliban had previously imposed restrictions on women's
clothing and appearance, this was the first decree to outline criminal
punishment for violations of the dress code.

Nilofar

I do not want to wear a burqa.

> **Zainab**
>
> You have a point, Parand jan.
>
> The Taliban have instructed men to enforce the hijab rule on women. This way, the domination of men in the home is strengthened and the Taliban's patriarchal utopia, critiqued for twenty years, is getting a fresh start. The Taliban's war with the people, especially the women of Afghanistan, has always been unfair, cruel and illegal. But now their sinister tricks have started a war inside homes.
>
> A woman can fight against the Taliban and protest against him as an outside enemy, but not against those men who are related to her, especially the men who have taken to the Taliban way of thinking. Covering women's bodies under the burqa is only part of the story; the main goal is to throw a burqa over women's thinking.

Nilofar

That's right.

Nilofar

Today was a very bad day. The kindergarten administration calculated that the number of students had decreased by half, and they contacted the families of the absent students. They found that the majority of parents were not sending their children due to fears for their safety. It is possible that, unable to operate on a reduced income, the kindergarten will close and we will lose our jobs. And the only thing that got us out of our houses. We will have nothing left.

Nilofar

Today the Taliban warned one of the teachers in our kindergarten that she did not have the correct form of Islamic burqa. The Taliban told her all the teachers must cover their faces and wear black clothes, or they would not be allowed to enter the school. We all are so upset and angry and worried.

> ### Batool, Rome, Italy
>
> I wouldn't give up under such pressure. If you can, even covering your face and wearing glasses, you should continue to protest this tyranny.

Nilofar

I covered my eyes with the burqa twice today, on the way to school and on the way back. Both times, I felt blinded. My eyes hurt. Many women are not used to this and for some women, like me, it is very difficult. The Taliban travel around in their fast cars; even their movement through the city scares us. They are spreading fear across the city.

Nilofar

Yesterday, when I was teaching religion, I told my students that some people pray with their hands by their sides, and some with their hands clasped on their chests. A student of mine said, 'Only infidels pray with their hands by their sides.' For a moment, I felt angry and confused. I said, 'I, too, pray with my hands by my sides.' My student laughed but also looked a little embarrassed. I didn't feel angry with the boy, but I was very angry with his parents and family. This is why our mosques are blown up – because, in their eyes, we are infidels.

Freshta, Dushanbe, Tajikistan

It has been raining since last night. The blossom in the trees is damaged, but the farmers are happy because this rain will bring prosperity. I had to go to the shops to buy my daughter some formula milk. I went out and waited to cross the street. A car passed, so I stood back to avoid being sprayed as it passed through puddles. But it was going very fast, and I got covered in mud and water, even up to my face. I was furious. I ran after the car, and the driver laughed at me. He said, 'This is not your country, you refugee. This is my land. I can drive the way I want to drive.' I told him I wasn't asking him to wash my clothes, but an apology would be nice, since he is a civilised citizen of Tajikistan. He replied, 'I did well and don't regret it. I would kick all you Afghans out of Tajikistan if I had the power.' I asked him what we had done to him. He said, 'We hate you. You have ruined your country, and now you come here to destroy ours. Look at you, walking in Western clothes. In Afghanistan, you'd have to wear a burqa. Just be thankful to God that we do not impose a burqa on you, don't expect apologies.' I turned away. I could not reply to him, but I cried about my situation.

ॐ

Batool

I feel that it is very difficult to understand the
people of Afghanistan. You will never understand
us unless you have been in our place. Our days are
filled with perplexity, wandering and asking
ourselves, *Why?* We are like a bird who flies to
find small perches even in wind and storms. She
cannot stop moving. She flies in search of greener
lands and bluer skies, and freedom. She feeds her
children and educates them. But then another
strong wind blows and breaks the branches of the
latest tree. The nest falls. She opens her eyes amid
bushes she has never seen, a stranger to herself.

Will this night turn into morning? Will the
window open, so we get to see the sun? The
bird, too, has closed her eyes, hoping there will
be a morning, for she has lost flight. Will she be
able to fly again with her broken wings?

*Batool and her family are living in a room in a Protestant church in
Rome. In exchange for their housing, they are given tasks: among
them, to keep the church and its grounds clean, and to wash plates
after church events. Batool's husband also works in a local bakery,
but it has not been easy to get the children properly into school.
Batool feels a little religious pressure too: she says, 'I left Afghanistan
to escape religion and now I'm under the thumb of religion again.'*

ॐ

Najla

Today is the third day that Kabul doesn't have electricity. These apartments all have modern toilets and bathrooms, and all the residents are trying to collect water to bring home. My son managed to carry a small container up to the third floor. He was out of breath. I felt sorry for him and wished that one container held enough water for the family. The electricity comes to Afghanistan from neighbouring countries and our government owes those countries money. I don't know what will happen if the debts are not paid. In the last forty-three years of war, the electricity and water supplies have been attacked. Only the government has changed; the war is still the same.

When I heard the new announcement about women needing to wear full hijab outside, I thought to myself: I am a Muslim woman. It was my identity even before the Taliban. I always wore a long hijab and headscarf and never showed my hair. Still, I never wore a full black hijab. I have always worn a headscarf in a decent colour. The Taliban prefer a full burqa. I spent the whole night thinking, what if a Talib stops me on the road tomorrow for not wearing a burqa? I don't want to go to work in a burqa. I am really worried and anxious.

Najla

We are all worried and anxious at home. We have to decide what to do. Today, I talked to my husband about finding a route out of the country. I spoke to my friends who lived in different parts of Afghanistan and asked them what their plan was. They replied that we are fenced like mice in a trap. We knew this hijab announcement would eventually come but did not expect it so soon.

The last time the Taliban took charge, my eldest son was twelve years old, and my eldest daughter was six – we only had the two of them then. We had to leave our country for their education. We became refugees and started from zero. When Hamid Karzai's interim government came, we returned to our homeland and started from zero again. Now, it looks as if we need to do it again. We'll have to sell our household goods to gather some money. But even those who were buying second-hand goods before are not buying anything any more.

Najla

Jets and helicopters are flying in the sky of Kabul. I looked out of the window but could not see any aeroplane. I went to check from the rooftop. I saw two helicopters and asked myself where they might be from. Since the Taliban came, I haven't seen helicopters in the sky. I cannot believe these belong to the Taliban. So, where are they from? It is very strange.

One of my friends, Zahira, rang me from Jalalabad in the afternoon. She said she also saw many helicopters in the air and jets flying in the sky. The news does not report these things, at least not inside Afghanistan.

I can't move, to walk into the light and touch the dewy new leaves of the quince tree. But then I remember there are migrating birds in the sky that need this liquid more. The Kabul summer is not far away.

Maryam

17
Working conditions
1–30 June

Work brings the writers some respite as they persist with life in Afghanistan and exile. The obstacles don't lessen.

Parand, Kabul

Today when I was coming home from work, I saw something that made me very sad. I got into the passenger van and took a seat at the very back, the only row of seats dedicated to women since the Taliban came. We spent a lot of time in traffic in a corner of the city near the ice cream bazaar. That's when I saw a woman in her chadari getting down from another passenger van, a little boy holding her hand. Within a minute, a man got out of the van and walked towards the woman. He raised his hand in the gesture of a slap and admonished her. 'Who said you could get out of the van without my permission? Go back inside . . .' These days it seems as if men kept their prejudices against women to themselves for twenty years and are now expressing them freely. There is no law to stop them.

Parand

I was talking on WhatsApp to my cousin, who lives in one of those Western countries, and she said, 'Since the Taliban took over Afghanistan,

whenever my husband is angry, he tells me that
if I behave in this way or that, he will buy me a
ticket and send me to Kabul.' Even Afghan men
living abroad are more inclined now to practise
domestic abuse.

Nilofar, Mazar-e-Sharif

Today, the Taliban placed a tiny metal booth at
the main entrance of Balkh University. They
stood one security guard there to search all the
students passing through the gate. He looked like
a shepherd trying to herd a huge flock of sheep
through a narrow passage: most students walked
past him without being searched. We laughed to
think this was the best idea the Ministry of
Higher Education could come up with!

Atifa, Herat

Through the efforts of one of my friends, we
have arranged an English class for young
schoolgirls to study the language. I teach them
the English I know.

*A friend in Italy told Atifa that she would help her with funds to
buy books and supplies to teach girls English. So, Atifa arranged
an informal class in her own home for twenty to thirty girls
between the ages of ten and seventeen. People in the village soon
learned this was taking place. With that came the risk of being
reported to the Taliban, so Atifa decided to end the classes for
the safety of her students and herself.*

Nilofar

The school that I work at has always been under
threat from the Taliban, even during the

republican era, because of its Shia ideologies. Many families transferred their children to other schools because they were afraid the school would be attacked. One of my university classmates asked me the other day, 'Aren't you afraid of working in this school?' I said, 'No.' And then we both remained silent.

Naeema, Kabul

Our school doesn't have hygienic toilets for girls and many girls find this so difficult. We have raised it with our management and asked for help to build new toilets. Two members of the Taliban authority came to school to address any issues. One of them asked a girl in Year 5 what problems there were at school. She was very scared and seemed to be counting her words before she spoke. We hoped she would talk about the toilets. Instead, she said, slowly, 'Schools are closed for girls above Year 6 and we are very worried.' I said to my colleagues, 'Here is a generation that knows what to demand. I am proud to be their teacher.'

Farangis, San Francisco, USA

After a long wait, I finally got a better job in my own field: the law. The job is stable and has a reasonable salary. I will start in a month's time, and I am so happy that I can finally send money to my family back in Kabul.

Farangis found a job working as a legal assistant with California's highway patrol, dealing with the laws that regulate the highways, the airways and shipping routes. This is the job for which she was interviewed earlier by a US army veteran who had served in Afghanistan. Although a qualified lawyer, she will have to pass the Bar exam for California before she is allowed to work as one.

Sadaf, Kabul

Sadaf continues working as a teacher, but with repeated closures she has also spent a lot of time at home this year. The class below is at one of the tuition centres common in Kabul.

Yesterday, during reading week, we made an exhibition of new books. There were lectures about the advantages of reading and our book – *My Pen Is the Wing of a Bird* – was mentioned. One of the students introduced the book in beautiful words. The best moment was when she mentioned my name and all my students cheered for me.

Naeema

Three years ago, I was involved in publishing ten books for children. Today, my biggest achievement is that I took a taxi alone.

Nilofar

People say the Taliban arrested Rajab Abrahimi, who is Hazara, for the crime of marrying a Pashtun woman. They claim that the marriage is haram, and their children are *haram-zada*, unlawful. I am very surprised by the silence of all these human rights activists. We are witnessing a violation of human rights and human dignity, and they are silent about it. Is humanity dead or what?

Parand

My husband and I are afraid of such a day.

Fakhta, Tehran, Iran

Che jaleeb, so interesting! Do you mean you and your husband are from two different ethnic groups?

Parand

Yes, my husband is Hazara and I am Pashtun.

Nilofar

Please be very careful, you two.

Fatima

I really don't understand this attitude. What is wrong with marrying between ethnic groups? Why are the Taliban so stupid?

Fakhta

So beautiful though! I wish you a happy and safe life together.

Parand

Thank you, Fakhta jan.

Nilofar

Parand jan, if you ever feel in danger, come to Mazar. Things are slowly getting better here. What I mean is that offices are open now. People go to work. Perhaps you can also find a new job for yourself here.

Parand

Tashakoor aziz-e-dil. Thank you, my sweetheart.

Danger seems to be inevitable for all Afghans since the birth of time. We are trying our best not to appear together too much and not to be recognised by anyone as husband and wife.

Masoma, Stockholm, Sweden

Masoma likes living in Sweden. She shares an apartment with another woman from Afghanistan who has been in Stockholm for years.

I've been taking a language course for the last four months. In our classroom, there are students from all around the world, with different faces, skin colours, belief systems and schools of thought. No one is related to anyone else.

To learn the language, we have started making simple sentences to introduce ourselves. For example, I say, 'I am Masoma,' and then I tell them where I live, where I've come from, and what language I speak.

Our teacher is an older woman with red hair. Her red hair makes me think of the novel *Anne of Green Gables* by Lucy Maud Montgomery. The first time our teacher introduced herself, I felt calmed by her questions. Then she asked:

'*Vad tycker du om?*' What do you like?

'*Vad tycker du inte om?*' What do you not like?

These last two questions are always very challenging for me to answer. I don't have one answer to these questions. So, I went silent. My mind filled with things I liked but had never had in life, and the things I had always had but had never liked. Then the teacher said, 'I don't like oppression,' and with this line a path opened in my throat. Yes, I, too, do not like oppression, bullying, violence, unkindness and thousands of other related things.

I like friendship. I like smiling. I like kindly looks. I like a heart you can trust. I love peace.

Nilofar

We were told, suddenly, to send our students home because of a storm coming. I thought this must mean there were some security issues. I said to myself, either there has been a suicide attack, or there is one coming. I sent my students home with a heavy heart, thinking it could be the last time I saw them.

I walked into the director's office and asked him, 'Is everything okay? Why did we have to send our students away?' He said, 'I don't know, they said because of some storm . . .' I said, 'What if something has happened, and we don't know yet?' He answered, 'No, I don't think so. They say the storm is going to be bad.'

For some reason, I was happy in my heart. Even if it is going to be a bad earthquake, still it will be a natural disaster. I am only afraid of human destruction, human disaster.

Fatima, Semnan, Iran

On the day I was to participate in York Literature Festival online, I had to wake up at 5 a.m. I took my father to the hospital for his eyes. He has cataracts from crying so much. At 8 a.m. they took him into the operating theatre. I was left alone in the hospital lobby, soon lost in thought. A woman came and kicked away my handbag, which I had placed next to my feet, before sitting down next to me. 'Are you okay?' I asked her. She seemed so angry with me. 'What am I to say? Your bag was in my way!' Then she mumbled to herself, 'They've come to our country and now they feel so entitled . . .' I didn't say anything, but I am so tired of this.

By 10 a.m. the operation was finished but it was 2 p.m. before we left the hospital. It took us another hour to get home and now there was only half an hour until my session at the festival. I tried to open the Zoom link, but my connection was not good enough. My mother suggested that I go to an internet café. I ran outside and took a taxi to the street with the internet shops, but many were closed. I ran to the only open one I could see. The people working there didn't allow me to use their computers because I was Afghan. They laughed at my accent. I headed back into town. I saw a little corner shop and thought I would try a different approach.

The shopkeeper was nice. I asked him if I could use his Wi-Fi for just a few minutes and I would pay him whatever it cost him. I finally got to join the festival and talked for a bit. When I finished, I thanked the man and tried to hand him some money, but he wouldn't take it. He only said, 'Take care, dokhtar jan. You are Afghan. The police might take you.' His kindness made me so happy. I was so happy I don't even remember how I got home.

Nilofar

Fatima jan, I wish your dad a speedy recovery.

Fatima

Indeed, thank you, Nilofar jan.

Najla, Kabul

I wish your father quick healing.

Fatima

Thank you, Najla jan.

Summer

18
Masoma's birthday
End of June

Masoma, Stockholm, Sweden

I've been wanting to write since my birthday. In
the last few months, I've found it very difficult to
write. Every time I tried, I would become
overwhelmed by the things I needed to write
about. I felt like someone who had been in love a
long time and suddenly lost their beloved. I
couldn't cry or scream because the pain was too
immense.

Even now, there is a congestion of words and
sentences in my head that do not allow me to
write fluently. But today I have decided to do it.
After a long time, today I bought myself flowers
and thought to myself that I must live. Like so
many of my friends and colleagues, I spent my
infancy, adolescence and early adulthood in
exile. But my life won't accept an end to my
wandering. Now, on my forty-eighth birthday, I
am a refugee again.

I've been alone most of my life – a never-ending
loneliness. I had this feeling even when I was in
Mazar or Kabul. In our society, women are seen
as burdens. We are seen as uninvited guests, as if
God created us to be humiliated. Even in your

own home, you feel you are an intruder. And that in society you're in the way. I felt this at university, at work, in the city, in the bazaar.

Once again, I am a refugee. It is very hard to be away from your home, your city, your memories, even from people who don't count you as equal. But when you have to flee for your survival, you go. The road to life in exile is long and dangerous. At times you are in worse danger than you were at home. But you gamble with your own life, hoping you will eventually find peace.

Like many other people, I made the decision to go as far from Afghanistan as I could. Now I am in a place where I don't look like anyone around me. I don't understand the language. I don't know my way around. I don't know people. It is possible that, in their eyes, I am odd and strange. By the way I dress, the way I sound, the way I eat, the way I look at people and things, the way I've learned everything I know, I am different. And here I must be born again, begin again.

For a long time as I walked, I felt I should apologise to everyone I saw in the street. Because I had come to their country without an invitation, without their permission. One day at the immigration office, I asked the official there for forgiveness.

During my interview with him, I said, 'I want to apologise to the people of Sweden for coming to

your country without permission. I am sorry to
be your burden. I don't have any claim on you.
Neither I nor my forefathers did anything for
your country. Whatever you've made of your
country is because of your own hard work. And
now we have come to bother you.' I felt my
emotion rise to my throat. With so much
kindness the man replied, 'It is every human's
right to live where they feel safe.'

He gave me a number for the police, to call if I
found myself in trouble. For the first time in my
life, I felt safe. I remembered all the fears in my
life, and then I thought about Farkhunda.*

I never knew how to complain when there was
no one to support me. And now these people
who don't know my language, and don't know
me, give importance to me and my security.
They care about where I live and whether I need
financial help. Here, I seem to mean something.

I remember one of the people who travelled with
me. She was from the Surobi district of Kabul.
She wasn't married and her parents had passed
away. Although she had siblings, she left them
behind and travelled all alone. Her Dari wasn't
good and we talked with difficulty. One day she
asked, 'Do you know why I am leaving the
country?' I replied that I didn't. She said, 'I don't

---

*Farkhunda Malikzada was a young woman who was publicly lynched by
a mob in Kabul on 19 March 2015, after being falsely accused of burning
the Quran. Her gruesome death sparked a wave of women's rights protests.

have anyone to take care of me when I am old and unwell. My brother and his wife are tired of me. I am going to Europe, so I am able to take care of myself.' That night we both cried together until morning. She talked about her life and I cried for all the pain we women have endured alone.

I cried because I couldn't do anything for the women of my homeland. I cried because I don't know how many more generations will have to endure injustice and violence like Farkhunda or be stoned to death like Rukhshana.*

---

*Rukhshana was stoned to death by a group of men in Ghor Province in 2015, after being accused of adultery. The man with whom she was allegedly eloping was let off with a lashing.

19
Waiting for rain

Early July

Sadaf, Kabul

I leaned my head against the window. I could hear the birds singing a pleasant melody. With every moment there was more light outside. Our life is indeterminate these days. We don't have any happiness to enjoy, yet we are not sad enough to take our own lives. It's as if we are all half alive and just want life to pass by quickly.

Sadaf

There should be some place, like a city for poor and hopeless people, so all the heartbroken people can gather there, in a dark room. We could book a ticket to go there when we feel sad and hopeless. Then the doors would be locked, and we could scream and shout for only the walls to hear. We could cry in that room and call anyone we wanted to speak with. We could spend as many days and nights there as necessary, to finally feel calm. I believe we need such a place.

Nilofar, Mazar-e-Sharif

Once again, the predictions have come true. War has begun in Balkhab district.* The people there may have a bloody summer.

Fatima, Semnan, Iran

Khuda raham kona. May God have mercy on us.

Masoma, Stockholm, Sweden

Today is 1 July 2022, and it is the second day that the Loya Jirga, the Grand Assembly, has been held in Afghanistan. I don't know if there is a foreign hand behind this council or not, but from what I see they are all insiders. This means these are the offspring of mothers living with them under the same sky. These delinquent children have gathered to make decisions about their mothers' lives and the country without the participation of their mothers, sisters or daughters. I am reminded of a household where the family gathers just like this, if on a smaller scale. The men decide the fates of mother, daughter, sister and wife, without their being included.

It makes me think about my mother's life, my own life and the lives of all the women of Afghanistan. It reminds me of all those women who stood up

---

*Mehdi Mujahid, a local Taliban commander, led a mutiny against the Taliban in Balkhab district. Mujahid's militia tussled with the Taliban for control of Balkhab, which the Taliban finally gained. Mujahid was killed in July. The number of civilian casualties and deaths is not known.

and resisted, to be driven away like me or crucified like Farkhunda. This dreadful council refreshes all the pains and wounds of my life.

I'm sure 99 per cent of this council is 99 per cent more backward in thinking and knowledge than the women whose lives they are legislating. The people who are making decisions about my life and the lives of all Afghan women, don't deserve to say one word about us. There is nothing in their filthy heads but ignorance and prejudice.

The poet said, 'Listen to me, and pray for him, even if he is not dead.' Now we must say, 'Pray for us women, not yet dead.'

Our situation is like the Jahiliyyah, the period of ignorance before the coming of Islam that is described in the Quran. Within the four walls of a house, they dig our graves and bury us alive. Our shroud is a cloth of misery. I don't know who handed it to us in this human place.

During her childhood in exile in Iran, Masoma listened to her mother tell stories of her homeland. They were not good stories, she says: they told her how hard life was for women in Afghanistan. As her mother's Alzheimer's progresses, she no longer remembers her own stories, but they are what originally inspired Masoma to write.

Masoma

In the year 1995, when there was an uproar about the coming of the Taliban, I wrote a short

291

story called 'Mand Ab', or 'Marshland', because I wanted to point out that all Afghan men are Taliban. It was the right conclusion too: I could feel the presence of the Taliban coming from faraway lands and also inside our home. To my father, his son who had no understanding, no education, no courage, no common sense, was still far better than me. Right before his death, he put my brother in charge of the family affairs, just as today those with no education, no understanding, no sense or humanity rule us, make it their role to guide us on *amr-bil-mahroof*, what is good.

I keep saying *maan*, I, but what I am really saying is *maa*, we. All our lives, all of us women, including myself and my mother, have been oppressed. And that's why we accepted the life we lived. The situation never changed for us because we brought our sons up like their fathers. They too believe that women are inferior to men in thinking and intelligence. They too think women are their property. They think women are soulless bodies, and thus we are to be enslaved. Today is the day of my death, you can now read me your final prayers.

Nilofar

The Taliban shot dead one of the residents in Balkhab. He was a frail old man. Wasn't it emphasised by the Prophet that women, children and the elderly should not be harmed in war?

What kind of religion is the Taliban preaching here? It seems the Taliban have used the name of Islam to frame a religion of their own to commit their crimes. I know there are many people at large who oppose the Taliban, but we can't sigh out loud or shed a tear for the poor and oppressed people of Balkhab. These crimes are happening to them because they are Hazara.

Nilofar

During Ramadan, I filled out passport forms for myself and my family. They told us that when the new batch of passports arrived, they would instruct us to go to Kabul to record our biometrics. The new passports are here and people with power or money or some connection with the government have already obtained their passports. But we have heard nothing. What is the difference between this government and the previous one, when corruption is intense in both? It's only the mask that has changed.

Fatima

In two days, it will be Eid al-Adha. Last year, during this Eid, the whole of Afghanistan drowned in blood and war. A lot of children became orphans, and many women became widows. During the same Eid, my brother, Hasan, who was in the military, was martyred in Herat. He went to his job and never came back. My uncle brought the news of his death. All of a sudden, we didn't belong to our home.

It has been a year since his death, and I still spend my days in disbelief, looking for a sheep to sacrifice. We are Afghans in Iran, and it is not easy to find sheep at a reasonable price. We were brought up to believe that if we sacrifice a sheep for the people we've lost, there is a *sawaab*, reward, for both those lost and those bereaved. I don't know any more if there is a problem with our culture, our religion or with me. I just know this: no one has an answer to all our torments and miseries.

Sadaf

We are strangers in our own land, Fatima, may God bless you.

Sadaf

It is Eid soon. I bought fabric to make an outfit for myself and also bought henna and bangles. But last night, going to bed thinking about my life and broken wishes, I shed tears on my pillow and gave up on making an outfit for Eid. I did not want to put henna on my hands. I remembered a song by Salih Mohammad Kandahari that asks, 'To whom shall I look and make my heart happy, to whom shall I complain about my life, to whom shall I show it by throwing dust on my head?' I am a strong person, but I cannot continue any more.

Parand, Kabul

It is getting more difficult to continue working, although the Taliban have not yet fully banned women from going to work. Parand and the other women in her office work segregated from their male colleagues.

Apparently, the Taliban want to streamline their government. Or, should I say, they want to eliminate women from government and other institutions. We had been advised by the Ministry of Economic Affairs that before starting any job we needed to get a work permit from the Ministry of Interior Affairs. Going there for the second time, I experienced extreme hopelessness. I'm sure all my female colleagues felt it too. It started from the entrance of the building. As we arrived, they asked why we were there. Then they said we couldn't enter the building without masks. They didn't mean we needed to wear masks for health reasons, they meant it as a form of hijab.

Each worker in the building kept asking why we were there. 'Where are you headed?' 'These women, where are they going?'

Once we entered the Directorate of Public Affairs, we had to queue for a very long time. Then they said, 'Based on the command of the Ministry of Interior Affairs, we cannot issue work permits to women yet.' The men in my office received their documents without any headache while we waited.

One of our male colleagues went to the office of the director and tried to talk to him. The director had told him, 'What do women do with a job? Why do they need a job outside their homes? They should stay inside their homes and do the household chores.' He then added, 'Women are the biggest hindrance and burden to our governance.' After a lot of placating, the ministry officials finally signed our documents. They said, 'Your team is the first female group in this field to get our permission to work. It's only because you connect with the health sector.'

We women sat outside feeling helpless until our colleague walked back from the office with the documents. After he told us what the director had said, our helplessness was replaced by humiliation.

Nilofar
Parand jan, these days shall pass.

> **Parand**
> I hope they do, Nilofar-e-aziz, dear Nilofar.

Freshta, Dushanbe, Tajikistan
Yesterday, my sister called me. I was out in Dushanbe city, so I did not pick up. I didn't want to speak while I was outside because we speak Pashto to each other. In Tajikistan, if someone hears us speaking Pashto, they will ask if we are part of the Taliban tribe. What does that even mean?

We have to remain silent. We are refugees. We came here to seek refuge from bad days and save our lives. If we had a chance to live in peace in our own country, we would not have anything to seek in this country. It pains me that I can't even answer my phone in public. The Taliban do not belong to any tribe in Afghanistan. They are the puppets of foreigners and do as they are told. They have damaged the reputation of Pashtuns more than any other tribe in Afghanistan. We are their enemies. Why can't I live in my country? Because of the Taliban, of course.

Freshta

Both of us are liars.

'What are your thoughts?'

'Nothing. I hope good news comes.'

I fall silent because I know what he means by 'good news'.

He hides things from me, and I hide things from him. We both worry, although it disturbs our sleep. He falsely comforts me, and I do the same for him. I try to convey that everything is all right, all will be fine, and we can live a happy life. We are both liars. Deep inside me, there is a worry that won't let me rest. Five months ago, we had a lovely daughter, but she doesn't have any documents. She doesn't have a passport, and right now it is so important to have an official identity.

I have been waiting to receive an email for 280 days now. This email will determine our future, especially my daughter's future. This is about my application to have our family resettled in a third country as refugees. They've told me that the application is being processed, but they

haven't said yes or no yet. If they would just
reply, I'd know what to do next. If my inner
world was filmed, the world would be shocked:
I cannot lessen my fears, I cannot go to
Afghanistan, and life is hard in Tajikistan.

My husband and I are both impatient to receive
this email. Whenever I get a notification, I
immediately look, but they are always just
Facebook notifications. I feel anxious and think
about what could happen if I received the email
and didn't notice. Even if I try to stop thinking
about it, I cannot. In reality, this email seems to
exist only in my head.

Nilofar

Since the fall of the government, I don't go to
Friday prayers. I've heard that the Taliban does not
allow Shia women to join in the Eid prayers. I say
to myself that we prayed so hard for the defeat of
the Taliban, but they were still victorious. We must
none of us be true believers, because God hasn't
accepted anyone's prayer yet. That's why I am not
going to Friday prayers any more.

Fatima

These days, I am very inattentive to everything. I
have no peace of mind and I go from one
thought to another. You could talk to me for
hours and I wouldn't understand a single word.

My mother befriended an Afghan neighbour some
time ago. She explained my state of distraction to
our neighbour. Today, the neighbour picked me

and my mother up at five o'clock, and we walked some twenty streets north.

We passed the old garment houses and walked down a dead-end street. We entered an old house and found it filled with Afghan women and their infants and other children. There was barely a spot for us to sit. An Afghan teacher was teaching the Quran. Each woman had to read the Quran out loud.

My turn came. I first had to recite a few verses of the Quran from memory before reading from the Book. The teacher was happy with my performance, and she asked me to sit for a test on Sunday. If I pass the test, I will be able to read the Quran with her at the classes.

It was a good day: I feel calmer and a little joy.

As we were walking back, I asked our neighbour why they had not chosen a better place in which to teach. The neighbour said, 'It is because she is an Afghan. She doesn't have permission to teach.' I think our Khanom Ma'elem, Madam Teacher, is like a fruit tree. No matter the weather, she offers her fruits.

It was a great day for me. I stepped out of my isolation, and finally, I am feeling better.

∞

Zainab, Abu Dhabi, UAE

It hadn't rained for six months and six days.
This may not sound significant. But when you
have lived your life with four vivid, changing
seasons of the year and then you suddenly find
yourself in a place where everything is the same
year-round, it affects your body and mind.

Yadesh bakhir, how good to remember the times
we had! Back in our homeland, the sky in spring
was vibrant, puffy clouds dancing above our
heads. Rain falling on the ground would bless us
with freshness and the smell of moist clay.
Earthy soil, green growth: we had it all, but still
we felt poor. Summer was hot in Kabul but not
as hot as here. Then in autumn the air would
chill, and rain dripped off yellow leaves. Winter
was like a serious old man who made us tremble
at his cold. But he was generous and scattered
snow to settle softly on us. In a whole winter
here, I have never seen snow falling, and it feels
as if part of my sadness is because of that.

Here, as they say, literally everything is artificial.
There is no soil. There is only sand. They've put
down palm trees for decoration. The children
have plucked off the bottom leaves and they keep
those leaves in their rooms.

The weather is always hot, but these days the
temperature has increased further. It's as if
they've held a magnifying glass over this land, to
focus the heat to a high pitch. During the day,

when you walk outside, you are assaulted by the stench of artificial green grass parched by the sun. That's why, at 46 degrees Celsius, no one goes out unless necessary.

You open the tap and boiling water flows out.

Because we are near the sea, the air is sultry. And in this area, there are also factories polluting the air. You go for a walk, even at night, and feel suffocated. There are nights when the intense smell of gas and fuel makes you feel as if this whole area is going to explode. The air is so thick here no one would ever be able to recognise you by your own smell.

Then today, after six months and six days, it rained. I sat in the rain, the air still warm and steamy. Children played and chased one another through the shower. Men and women slowly emerged from their rooms to watch. But the weather still feels heavy – maybe it is the weather in my heart.

> Najla, Kabul
>
> Zainab *jan-e nazaneen*, dear sweet Zainab, it has been a long time since you last wrote in the diary. I'm so glad to see you here, safe and writing again. Thank you – you've written this so beautifully.

Zainab

You're so welcome, Najla *gul o mahraban*, kind like a flower. I've slowly started working on a longer story. Apart from more nostalgia and homesickness, nothing else is new here. Thank you for all your warm encouragement.

Zainab

By the way, Eid Mubarak to you all, and to your loved ones.

> **Nilofar**
>
> Salam everyone, and Eid Mubarak.

Naeema, Kabul

I too wish you a happy Eid. I hope you have a good day.

> **Najla**
>
> Thank you, Zainab jan. Also, Eid Mubarak to you and to all of you, my dear writer friends.

Atifa, Herat

Dostan-e-aziz, Eid Mubarak. Hope you're having a good day.

> **Fatima**
>
> Salam everyone, Eid Mubarak.

Maryam, Kabul

Salam, Najla jan, Eid Mubarak to you and everyone else.

> **Najla**
>
> Thank you, Maryam jan.

Masoma

I would also like to say Eid Mubarak to all of
you and wish you happy days. I pray to God that
on this holiday he brings an end to the misery of
our land and people. Ameen.

Farangis, San Francisco, USA

Today, on the first of Eid, we went to a friend's
home. As I was busy feeding my son, one of my
friend's daughters, who is five years old, came to
me and asked, 'Khala, do you have brothers and
sisters?' I thought perhaps this little girl could
sense my loneliness. Maybe she noticed that
while everyone else was talking and laughing, I
was not. I told her, 'Yes, I have one brother and
three sisters.' 'Where are they?' she asked. 'In
Afghanistan.'

The girl went away. But her question worked like
salt on my wounds. I got lost again in thoughts
of my family. I've always felt lonely here and
separated from my family, but this feeling has
now enveloped my existence. I can't think of
anything but them.

Nilofar

Our family and two other families went out for
the day, to the Sholgar River. The rice fields were
green all around and the river was full. It's a
popular place for picnics, just off the main road
between districts. Today the roadside was busy
with men, it was hard to spot a family. We
worried that, because of the large crowd of men,

women wouldn't be allowed down to the river, which it has been my long-time wish to visit.

But, with some effort, we found a nice corner for ourselves. My brother and the other men in our party asked us to come swimming with them. At first, I was hesitant, unsure of how to take such a step after being so long confined. But slowly we waded in to join them. It was a very special moment for me, the first time I had been in a river; the water fresh and soothing after all our troubles.

As we got out, now feeling the chill in the cold air, we saw two Taliba with weapons in hand leaving their black Corolla car and walking towards us. We were so afraid that they would take us to task for going in the water. But, to our surprise, four women and three children followed them. They'd parked their car next to ours and I slowly understood they were coming to join us, because we were also a family party.

Despite Taliban codes of hijab, the women were not wearing the niqab or chadari, or any sort of complete covering. They had long dresses on and long headscarves. The women didn't go in the water, but they took pictures. The men gave their Kalashnikovs to their kids and took pictures of them holding the weapons. This particular scene looked very frightening to my eye, but my brother said he'd also held guns in pictures as a child. They watched the river quietly, but we laughed out loud and screamed at times.

When we were preparing to leave, they also left in their car. I watched them and thought to myself that maybe with the passing of time they would change too. I think we were all thinking it. Perhaps one day they will let women be free.

20

The anniversary of the fall approaches

16 July–14 August 2022

Maryam, Kabul

I am in my wheelchair in our yard. Through the leaves of our quince tree, I'm looking at the stars. It is a bright night. The moon, the stars, the lamps: they all glow within the walls of our yard, adding to the light of the city. The tree shakes with the soft wind that blows. I'm talking to my brother and sister about the talk that girls' schools will reopen. I've been looking for news articles to confirm these rumours. But I haven't found any yet. I'm waiting for morning to see what will happen next.

I first heard the rumour from another woman. She was very hopeful. I couldn't bring myself to tell her we couldn't be sure unless the news was issued officially. Deep in my heart, I long to hear this announcement too, that's why I didn't want to kill her hope. I remember the first rumours about the fall of Kabul and how I saw them come true with my own eyes. Kabul fell a month later and I turned my back on the stars. I didn't want to look them in the eye.

Now, I stretch my hands towards the tree. This calm night, this cool breeze: they are here for the summer, and I want to let them in.

Sadaf, Kabul

Maybe I have got used to it. Perhaps I really can manage the lowest points of my life and hide my worries from the outside world like a secret. I am not ashamed to show my sadness, but I don't want to make anyone else sad. Sometimes, on my way to work, I cry alone. No one at work realises that I am upset, because now I know how to hide my sadness. I always wonder, will the day come that girls like me can escape this devastating situation? When we can actually be young girls and enjoy our lives? God forbid, maybe never.

Marie, Viersen, Germany

Today, I was talking with a German person. He asked me about my family and what they were doing, and the conversation came around to how I arrived in Europe. I asked his opinion about the current war between Russia and the West and when it would end. He sounded very sad. 'I don't like to say this, but there is another kind of war on the way, not only in Europe but the whole world.'

Nilofar, Mazar-e-Sharif

War has its cruelty. But predictions of the war leave us paralysed.

Marie

It is true. But for people like us, who are from Afghanistan, this kind of news is never new. At times we can be indifferent too. It is because we have always been helpless.

Maryam

I am reminded of the song, 'Salam Aleek', by Farhad Darya. I keep thinking to myself that, instead of other countries bringing their peace to our land, our land's war is spreading to theirs. When I see the state of the world as it is, I think to myself, if war is waged by low and selfish people, then what role do ordinary people play, who don't desire war? Are they spectators? Victims? Or wanderers? These are hard and bitter days. I hope politics change and war does not happen.

Parand, Kabul

The heat is raging in Kabul. People can neither sleep nor relax. Maybe it's because more people have come to the city or maybe it's the world's reckless attack on nature that has done it.

Farangis, San Francisco, USA

After my prayers today, I raised my hands to implore. '*Khuda-ya*, O God, bring prosperity and peace to my homeland.' These are words I heard my elders pray when I was a child. As I grew up, I recited the same memorised words. It is still one of my most important prayers.

Maybe God is tired of hearing the same words over and over. Maybe he doesn't want to hear this prayer any more. Should I stop saying it? Maybe God does not like repeated words and that is why our prayers for our homeland don't reach the heavens.

Golden stars on each branch of the tree, absorbing the summer. You could say these quinces have taken the last glow left in the city.

Maryam

Zainab, Abu Dhabi, UAE

We are approaching the first anniversary of *soqoot-ma'an*, our fall. The fall of Afghanistan, the fall of dignity, the fall of hope and life. We saw chaos and panic erupt a few days before the fall. No one's life has been the same since. I remember the day before the fall, when I looked out the window of a passenger van and saw the queue outside the bank stretching down the street, past many shops. I saw an awakening misery on the faces of people.

My friends – anyone working in an office – no longer went to work. Instead, they stayed at home and packed their belongings. Some people collected up their documents. All the internet cafés were full of people registering for passports online. The passport website itself crashed under the strain. People who weren't able to plan an escape went to shops and bought enough food to last for a while. Everything was getting more and more expensive. If you asked the shopkeeper why, he would say, 'The US dollar has gone up and the Afghani is losing value. I am making losses here too.'

On the day of the fall, people could be divided
into two main groups. There was the group
trying to get home and the group trying to get to
the airport. Inside their homes, people felt
hopeless, waiting for the phone to ring. Outside,
people faced fear and imminent death, hanging
onto the wings of planes.

The saddest part of all that has happened is
where we are now. The Taliban are practised at
oppressing people, and we have got into the
habit of accepting oppression. Even the world is
in the habit of watching oppression.

Batool, Rome, Italy

They were rough days. My husband and I
couldn't sleep till morning, reading the news. We
tried our best to keep the news hidden from our
youngest daughter.

I wanted to join the protests. It was agreed no
one would announce the location of our
gathering until the morning of the protest. We
all had to message this one woman to find out
where to go. I called her many times, but the
lines were not working. So, I went to try on my
middle daughter's phone. She was asleep. I
picked up her phone, its cover pink with purple
flowers. I opened her WhatsApp to message my
protesting group. But there I came across her
classmates' group chat. The whole group had
been sharing their stress, tears and worries over
WhatsApp. My daughter's classmates, thirteen
and fourteen years old, shared news of the

Taliban's arrival. They had also shared pictures of old men with long shirts, long beards and covered heads. Each one of them expressed their fears. 'If the Taliban comes for us, where should we go?'

I felt a lump inside my throat. My daughter was still asleep. I looked at her innocent face and promised myself I wouldn't let anything happen to her or her future under the Taliban flag. No matter how or when, I would take her out of the country.

Two days later, one of the girls' mothers deleted the chat group. All that was left of their chats now was the fear.

Nilofar

Today, there were many Taliban at the entrance of Kabul Bank – they were probably collecting their salaries. It reminded me of earlier times, during the republic, when we would see Afghan soldiers in their military uniforms lining up outside the bank to receive their salaries. I always worried an enemy would infiltrate the queue and commit a suicide attack.

I moved cautiously past the Taliban queue, hoping they wouldn't notice the way I wore my hijab. Yadesh bakhir, I remember the good times. I was never afraid of the army in this way, in their uniforms with tilted green berets. If anything, their presence made us feel safe and secure. We were proud of them.

It makes me so sad to think what must have
happened to each one of them. Perhaps the ones
who were martyred are blessed not to have seen
this disgrace of history.

Sadaf

Today I have felt upset since I woke up. The
situation makes me anxious. I want to be positive
and throw my negative thoughts out the window.
I want to write something optimistic, but even my
pen is strange. It only writes what I feel.

Sadaf

Oh, watan-am, watan-am, my homeland, who
cursed you? My heart aches. Afghanistan is
dead and its body lies there with no one to bury
it.

Marie

Oh, how I miss Bamyan.

Parand

Oh Azizam.

&

Fatima, Semnan, Iran

On the first of Muharram, it will be the
anniversary of my brother's death.

Parand

May his soul rest in peace.

Fatima

Thank you, Parand jan.

> **Atifa, Herat**
>
> Fatima jan, *rohash-shaad*, may his soul be
> content.

Marie

Khuda rahmat-ash kona. May God bless him.

> **Fatima**
>
> Tashakor, everyone.

Nilofar

Every year in the month of Muharram, the
whole city of Mazar and its suburbs were
flooded with mourning flags.* Everyone would
display black, green and red flags in their
streets. Even last year, when we were losing
province after province, the main streets and
squares of Mazar-e-Sharif were filled with
Muharram flags.

But this year, it is rare to see a mourning flag.
In some public places, the Taliban have
explicitly forbidden it. Elsewhere, they stand
guard so people don't dare. The basis of
Shi'ism and its ideology is Muharram and the

---

*Shia Muslims observe the month of Muharram as a period of mourning
to commemorate the martyrdom of Prophet Mohammed's grandson,
Husayn ibn Ali, in the Battle of Karbala. It is among the Shia traditions
suppressed by the Taliban.

mourning of Imam Hossein. And now the Taliban have tied the hands of Shias with these restrictions. There are no flags and no loudspeakers to play lamenting songs for Hossein. Even the cars do not play these lamentation songs.

This year's Muharram is sadder than any other year.

Naeema, Kabul

There is nowhere to cry. Today I left an apology letter at the school, stating that I could not return. It was not easy to decide that and say goodbye to my colleagues who had been family to me. They laughed with me when I was happy and cried when I was upset. As I left the school one last time, I said goodbye to all the other staff. I cried all the way home.

These days I want to escape to a calm and distant place where I can cry my heart out, but there is no such place. I have lost my job, my students, my colleagues, my friends, my purpose in life, my home and my country.

Naeema has just learned that she can leave Afghanistan with her sister, to begin life as refugees in Germany. They leave the following week.

Nilofar

Today, the Taliban took away the mourning flags for Hossein in Mazar-e-Sharif. Gathering up the

flags before the tenth day of Muharram is an
insult to those observing the Ashura.*

Nilofar

They even collected the flags displayed on lamp
posts on the Kabul–Mazar Road.

> **Freshta, Dushanbe, Tajikistan**
> Today my daughter cut her first tooth. My
> friend told me to throw a party, so we could
> gather and celebrate this happy moment. I don't
> have happy feelings. This is the month of
> August. Since the first day of August, I have felt
> strange. I feel as if I am breaking apart.
>
> My daughter was born exactly six months after
> the Taliban took over Afghanistan, just as I was.
> I was born in March 1997, and my daughter was
> born in February 2022. She is six months old,
> and still my baby doesn't have identity
> documents and we can't get her any. How can I
> be happy, how can I arrange a party?
>
> Today I looked into my daughter's eyes and
> promised her that things would change for us. I
> will fight for her to have a better life, no matter
> where I am. I cannot accept this gradual death. I
> will fight for girls' and women's rights, I won't
> be silent. The Taliban do not count me as
> human, they want to vanish me. And I do not

---

*Ashura is the tenth day of Muharram and is a day of commemoration
observed differently by Sunni and Shia Muslims. For Shias, the day is
marked with public displays of mourning.

count myself as Taliban. I believe that I am
fearless and that the talent and patience I have,
most men do not have. If men had suffered as
much as the women of my country have
suffered, they would have vanished. History has
proven that women are more potent than men.
From birth, I have struggled while men are given
every opportunity. I am sure one day women will
win. History will remember this.

Marie

Today is the tenth of Ashura, and I'm ever more
anxious. I don't know if our prayers are
answered. But from the bottom of my heart, I
pray that today goes well. I sent a message to my
mother this morning, but she hasn't received it
yet. I heard that they disconnected the internet
in the west of Kabul and only a few people have
access to the internet today. I don't know what
to do with all my stress and anxiety. I just pray
to God to protect those joining the Ashura
ceremony, so they can return home safely.

When I look around this world I live in now –
the people in Germany and their culture – it
makes me cry for my situation and our people's.
All these years, our minds have been preoccupied
with how to survive. We've always carried that
heavy burden of anxiety and fear – in which
suicide attack would we or our loved ones die?

Freshta

Today someone said to me that when Afghan
women come to Europe, or any free country, the

first thing they do is remove their headscarves.
She said it sarcastically. I told her, 'The women
of Afghanistan cannot even breathe freely, let
alone remove their scarves. When they are out of
that geography, they take a breath and start a
new life.' In Kabul, I wore a headscarf all the
time – at home, at school and at work. I wished
to live the way I wanted and remove my
headscarf. To breathe fresh air and wear
something that fit me properly, not two sizes
larger. But women are told to anticipate how
society will react and live accordingly.

Maybe in other parts of the world, people have
higher hopes. In Afghanistan, my only wish was
to cut my hair, wear jeans and have no one
comment on these things in the street. In
Tajikistan, I enjoy the breeze and listen to music
when I go for a walk. A few days ago, I
interviewed a girl who had been wearing a
headscarf for a decade because society obliged
her. She studied for many years in full burqa. She
said her biggest wish was one day to walk in the
street without fear and ride a bicycle without
anyone judging her. Her wishes were like mine.
When I see women from Afghanistan walking
free abroad, I am pleased. I hope one day all
women will break free from the prisons of
tradition and live the lives they want to live. It is
not essential to wear a scarf, but it is crucial to
live free.

Fatima

These days I am free, but not liberated.

I don't belong anywhere.
I don't have a place in my own country,
nor in the country of other people,
My feet hover above the ground,
my hands stretch towards a sky I can't reach,
I am free only in that sense.

Farangis

For several days now, whenever I raise my hands
in prayer, instead of praying, I question God. I
ask why he has not answered my prayers for
myself, my family and my country.

Last August, when the Taliban took over
Afghanistan, I was expecting my first child. I
will never forget that when I was taken to the
hospital for his birth, I carried my laptop in my
hand. I was hoping to find some calm time in the
hospital, to search for ways to get my family out
of Afghanistan. I feel even worse now than I did
then – everything I feared happened, and I only
watched it happen, unable to do anything about
it.

They say, without God's will, not even a leaf
leaves its tree.

Masoma

In three days, it will be 15 August, one year
since the collapse of Kabul. The anniversary
has already passed for Mazar and the northern
provinces. In the aftermath of the Russian
invasion and civil wars, and then the Taliban's
first takeover of Afghanistan, it can safely be

said that those twenty years were almost a golden period for the people of Afghanistan. Those were the years when people were able to heal the wounds of past years, despite suicide attacks and government corruption. Suddenly, when no one was paying attention, we fell together. Not only did the young man fall who clung to the wing of a plane, but the whole map of Afghanistan fell from the geography of the Earth. With this fall, each one of us fell. All that we had built with a thousand hopes, despite a thousand struggles – it all broke with the fall.

From far away, we read the news and hear stories. We see videos of beheadings, news of a girl being murdered by her father or brother, news of someone committing suicide, news of men forced into prostitution, news of refugee boats sinking in the sea, news of a migrant being tortured at the border, news of someone selling his kidney or his child. On and on it goes. All day we follow the news and at night we wonder what kind of doctor to visit tomorrow for the things that ail us. Those who left the country are dealing with a mountain of problems, and those who remain in the country are unsure of their future, even their lives.

Nilofar

The Taliban has declared tomorrow a public holiday. They are going to celebrate the day on which all our dreams and hopes collapsed.

Maryam

Yes, tomorrow, there will be a celebration of the anniversary of unemployment, poverty and hunger in the country of incompetence and purposelessness. What is the need for a holiday? Apart from the Taliban and a few others, who else has jobs and duties?

It feels as if that day is happening again. I feel uneasy, frightened and without hope. Now we have lived a whole year in defeat, why am I still afraid?

I touch the lowest branch of the quince tree to pick a sweet golden fruit. I am still too short, sitting in my wheelchair. I know others have left and moved on to another country to be safe. I cannot even reach this tree. I will see it without fruit, standing alone against the autumn winds – I will see it turn yellow, then without leaves, then with blossom.

Maryam

About the writers

January 2024

Atifa

Atifa travelled to Iran a month after the close of this diary, with her mother, sisters and youngest brother, as they had contemplated doing for some time. They live in Mashhad, one of Iran's larger cities, close to the border with Afghanistan. Atifa struggles to find work because her qualifications are not recognised. She hopes to work further on her English and apply for a scholarship to study in another country. She tries to keep writing.

Batool

Batool left Italy with her family, after a year, to seek asylum in the UK. They are living in a hotel housing refugees outside Oxford. 'It's a good place,' Batool says, 'maybe you would not find it so, but it's good for me right now.' She is happy that at last her children are in school. Batool spends her own time offering free online therapy to teenage Afghan girls from Mazar, Kabul and Baladakhshan who can no longer go to school. But she does not feel safe yet and finds it impossible to think about the future.

Batool's short story, 'The Grey Winged Pigeons of the Shrine', is scheduled to be published in translation from Dari in *Words Without Borders* in March 2024.

Elahe

Elahe has given up trying to find work, after routinely being paid less because she is Afghan. She is focused on learning German, with hopes of migration from Iran. She is also teaching herself to play the guitar, following YouTube tutorials.

Fakhta

Fakhta and her husband are still in Iran. They have moved from Tehran to a suburb, where they live in a room in an apartment block where her husband works as a security guard. Fakhta now works as a sales assistant in a grocery shop. They earn enough to eat and cover their rent, she says, but it is not a full life, just survival. When Fakhta comes home from work, she sleeps for a few hours so she can spend some time writing in the middle of the night.

Farangis

Farangis had to leave her job with the California highway patrol, to her great disappointment, because there was no one to look after her son and she didn't earn enough to justify the cost of childcare. She and her husband live in the Bay Area of San Francisco but now struggle to keep up repayments on their mortgage, with just one salary coming in. Her husband continues to support her writing, and she shares her work with him.

Farangis's short story, 'The Emergence of Power', was published in translation from Dari in *Moveable Type* in 2023.

Farishta

Farishta lives in an apartment in Ottawa, Canada with her mother and sister. She is curious about her new surroundings and does not feel demoralised about the need to start again. She has completed a conversion course that allows her to begin an MA in Public Policy and Administration, focusing on Child Development. Meanwhile, she works for an advertising company and is still writing stories in Pashto. She intends to translate these stories into English herself.

She rejoined the Untold writers' group in September 2023.

Fatima

In Iran, Fatima has held a series of jobs for short periods, including as a flower seller and in the office of an insurance company. She is now employed by a company that packs and distributes coffee and powdered soft drinks. She works in the packing section and is much happier now, as the owner of the company is a kind person. She says in Iran, although the authorities are hostile, it is possible to survive because you find good people who will help you.

Fatima shares her short stories with her mother and father. Her short story, 'The Greenhouse', is scheduled to be published in translation from Dari in *Words Without Borders* in March 2024.

Freshta

Since August 2022, Freshta has been working again, which has brought her relief. She is a journalist and editor for the Zan Times News Agency. Her husband never managed to find work as a journalist and, after he was twice injured on the construction sites where he worked, Freshta suggested that he stay at home and look after their daughter so she could work more hours. They did finally receive the email they were waiting for, inviting them to submit biometrics towards an application for resettlement. They are still in Tajikistan, now waiting for the next email.

Marie

Marie still lives in Bad-Berleburg, a market town in Germany. She describes it as a beautiful, calm place where people are nice. She still attends daily language classes: she has enough

German to get by, but not enough to work. She's joined a cycling group. She would love to run a business of her own eventually.

Marie's short story, 'The Café', was published in translation from Dari in *Moveable Type* in 2023.

Maryam

Maryam is still at home in Kabul with her family. Rarely able to leave the house, she immerses herself in books and music. Each morning she selects a new book to read and, if it is good, she reads all day. She writes or makes notes for writing.

Her short story, 'Kabul's Haikus', was published in translation from Dari in *The Markaz Review* in 2023.

Masoma

Masoma is happy living in Sweden and agrees with what she'd been told: that it is a good country for single women. She still attends daily language classes, although she can manage life in Swedish now. She is taking a course that will help her convert her engineering qualifications for use in Sweden. She looks forward to working as an engineer and hopes also to start work on a novel.

Mehrsa

Mehrsa left Iowa for Maryland because she had visited and found it a more diverse area, with a larger Afghan community nearby. She completed the last semester of her master's degree from there and now works at George Washington University, in the administration of the careers section.

Mehrsa's short story, 'Broken Branches', was published in *Moveable Type* in 2023.

Naeema

Naeema now lives in Berlin with her sister, while her brother remains in Kabul with his family. They live in a refugee camp outside Berlin, attending daily German-language classes. Naeema knew, from relatives' stories, to expect a difficult life but the thing that overwhelms her is the shortage of housing. She has spent over a year looking for a one- or two-bedroom apartment to rent. She is trying to write, but misses her old life as a teacher.

Najla

Najla says of Kabul that it is her life: however much she writes about Kabul, it is never enough. She hates the idea of leaving her home, but now feels perhaps she must, for the sake of her children and grandchildren. She is full of anxious thoughts these days. At the moment, even the park is closed to women.

Her short story, 'The Blue Sky of Kabul', was published in translation from Pashto in *Psyche* in 2023.

Nilofar

Nilofar and her brother and sister finally did get passports and left to live in Iran as refugees again. They hoped their stay in Iran would be short, and they might proceed to another country, but they were in Iran eight months, living in a small hotel in Tehran, unable to work. Nilofar kept in touch with Atifa and Fatima, also recent arrivals in Iran, but they lived in three different cities and could never meet. Nilofar and her siblings left Iran in the last days of 2023, and have just arrived in Islamabad, Pakistan.

Nilofar's story, 'Continue Watching', was published in translation from Dari in the Winter 2023 issue of *Brick* magazine.

Nora

Nora and her family managed to move to Germany after seven months in the refugee camp in Spain. They are in Hamburg and are happy to be there. The children already speak very good German and Nora now feels comfortable operating in German, though she continues to strive for the next level of language qualification. Once she has this, she will be able to apply to a medical school to find out how many years of study she will need to convert her medical qualifications. She hopes that in three years' time she will be able to work again as a doctor. The family lives in central Hamburg and Nora's parents and sisters also live in the city. She still writes. That's what keeps her going, she says.

Parand

Parand is now living in Kunduz with her husband. They are increasingly careful to keep a low profile; Parand dresses in full black chadari and tries not to be seen much in public. She is still able to work: she and all her female colleagues must work from home now, although their working days are disrupted by long power cuts. Parand struggles with the restrictions on her freedom. She continues writing under her long-term pen name, Parand, sometimes feeling sad that none of her creative work has ever appeared in her own name.

Her short story, 'Breaking News', was published in translation from Dari by *Critical Muslim* and in *Moveable Type* in 2024.

Rana

Rana and her family live in a large house in Melbourne that can fit them all, very happy to have been able to stay together. They now have permanent residency in Australia. They found it strange at first needing to smile and say hello to people on the street – even men! – although there was no one they really knew in Australia but each other. Now, they are slowly getting used to the local customs, attending English classes and also meeting other Afghans in Australia. Rana is teaching Pashto to Afghan women, on a voluntary basis. Once she has completed her English classes, she hopes to find paid work, and is determined to keep writing. Rana turns thirty this year.

Sadaf

Sadaf still lives in Kabul. She continues to work as a teacher, a job she loves, now teaching girls and boys in primary school. She is newly married, after an eight-month engagement. During her engagement, she was apprehensive about what married life would be like, but now she is very happy. It's going well.

Samira

Eleven months after she arrived in France, Samira gave birth to her first child. She is in Bordeaux, France, with her husband and young son. It has been difficult to continue her French-language classes with a baby, but she tries to keep learning on YouTube. She likes to go to the seaside whenever she can. Girls don't get taught to swim in Afghanistan, she says, but she finds it calming just to walk along the beach, watching the sea. Samira hopes to go back to university one day and, with all the professors of Persian literature in France, to learn to read and translate Rumi.

She rejoined the Untold writers' group in 2023.

Zainab

In September 2022, Zainab and her husband were able to travel onward from the camp in Abu Dhabi, becoming refugees in Abbotsford, British Columbia, Canada. Zainab likes Canada. She feels it is a place where multiculturalism and freedom are in practice; people are allowed to bring their cultures with them and be themselves, she says. It's a lovely city she lives in, too, with trees everywhere and clean air. She's learning English, which she hopes will help her find a job. Her husband, who was a video editor back in Afghanistan, is currently working installing shelving in supermarkets. Zainab volunteers as an interpreter and translator for other Afghan refugees who are struggling. She hopes one day to write in English, too, but will begin with stories of Aghan women and girls because, she says, those stories aren't over yet. She still writes every day.

Zainab's short story, 'The Hotel', was published in translation from Dari in *Pen Transmissions* in 2023.

೮ಾ

Two books of the group's collective writing have been published previous to this one. They are My Pen Is the Wing of a Bird *(MacLehose Press, 2022) and* Rising After the Fall *(Scholastic, 2023).* My Pen Is the Wing of a Bird *was a finalist for the Jan Michalski Prize 2022 and has been translated into Korean, Japanese and Ukrainian. The writers continue to meet regularly as a group.*

Translator's Note

In *One Way Street*, Walter Benjamin argues that 'The power of a country road when one is walking along it is different from the power it has when one is flying over it by aeroplane. In the same way, the power of a text when it is read is different from the power it has when it is copied out.' As a translator of Afghan literature, I like this analogy of copying, or indeed translating, a book with walking the landscape of a country rather than flying over it. There is a particular truth to this image, because the landscape of Afghanistan has typically been portrayed to the rest of the world as seen from above and afar. But in *My Dear Kabul*, twenty-one writers give the world a walking person's account of Afghanistan's alleys, lanes, ponds and mud flats, where both horror and hope reside.

In October 2022, after a session on short stories by Afghan women at the Birmingham Literature Festival, Lucy Hannah, from Untold Narratives, asked about my interest in a translation project based on a thread of messages between twenty-one Afghan writers after the fall of Kabul. I knew a few of the women from my previous translation work with Untold for the anthology *My Pen Is the Wing of a Bird* (MacLehose Press, 2022). I realised both what this project would entail and the inherent power in the collective voice of these women writers. When I first started reading these messages weaving through the year, I was overwhelmed. Here was one woman's hope, another's despair, one woman's love and kindness, another's disturbance. Then, there were moments of sheer literary brilliance – in both Dari (Farsi/

Persian) and Pashto – oscillating between everyday conversation and poetry.

Dari and Pashto are the two official languages of Afghanistan. Both are written in the Arabic alphabet, from right to left. Almost half of the population in Afghanistan speaks Dari in different dialects, such as Herati, Kabuli and Khorasani Dari. However, the language is used well beyond Afghanistan: there is Iranian Yazd Dari and Kerman Dari, as well as a small group of Dari speakers in Pakistan. Within Afghanistan, the Dari speakers are either Tajiks, Hazaras or Chahar Aimaq people. Unlike many other Indo-European languages, Dari does not distinguish between genders: men, women, animals and objects share similar nouns and pronouns. When translating Dari into English, these obscurities, woven into grammar and syntax, can either be desperately limiting or extremely liberating, especially in terms of character and situation.

Pashto, by contrast, differentiates gender; the distinction is found in a word's ending. While Pashto is also a member of the Iranian group of Indo-European languages, in matters of grammar and syntax it is slightly different from Persian (Dari). Pashto is widely spoken by the Pashtun people in Afghanistan and parts of Pakistan, and it became the second national language of Afghanistan in 1936. As someone growing up in a Dari-speaking household, learning Pashto was always a priority for me. Similarly, for someone growing up in a Pashto-speaking household, to learn Dari was a common choice. As a translator of Dari and an editor of Pashto, one thing has become clear to me: both languages are equally expressive, each with its unique poetic tendencies, literary histories and cultures.

Any written work of art becomes comprehensible with a deeper understanding of its form. The form, in this case, is something between epistolary exchange and journal-keeping. But the more I understood the form, the more complex, unique and challenging the task became. My previous translation work had been

with classical and medieval Persian poetry and prose for schol-
arly purposes, or contemporary essays about Afghanistan,
modern Dari (Persian) poetry, and short stories. Each was the
work of a single author. For this project, I had to navigate the
words of twenty-one writers from different backgrounds and
walks of life. How to remain true to each writer's voice and style,
as they appear in the original? More importantly, how best to
translate a work of such collective power?

It is not surprising that the writer's personalities and literary
preferences become distinctive when they are expressing deep
fears and a changing reality around them. Some prefer short
sentences like the lines of a poem; some write with a reporter's
diligent description; others provide longer analytical accounts,
like a teacher, or psychologist. I have tried to retain the original
form of their messages as far as possible. Line-to-line messages
were easiest to translate. Those that resembled a poem took
some thought. But once I decided to keep the original form of
each entry, verses became easy to translate. In such segments, I
felt that the writer had permitted me to include the spaces where
beauty and fear are experienced together. Sometimes the same
writer would send messages seconds or minutes apart; I did not
dare to disturb the emotion reverberating through the sequences
of those words. I inserted a space after each message, both to
respect the breaks in the writer's entries and to indicate to the
reader that there had been such a break.

In the first stage of translation, it was necessary to retain
longer passages in the form of reportage. However, in the second
stage, more editorial shaping was sometimes essential to translate their meaning. Through the various forms of expression,
every emotion is shared; these writers rarely censor themselves.
In translating their accounts, my task was more than just convey-
ing their words in English: I wanted to convey the
magnitude of their bravery and power. As much as getting the
translation right, I was concerned about capturing the tone and

feeling of every situation they described. Between the source language and the target language, there is always an in-between moment, when the translator stops typing and waits for the soul to settle. For me, these in-between moments came when the bravery and resilience of these women spoke louder than history. Amid the emotional exchanges, there are moments of colloquial essence, especially when it comes to writers expressing their despair, anger and frustration. I decided not to translate some of these – moments so sacrosanct they should only be shared between the writers at that particular moment.

In places, I retained the Persian or Pashto words to convey these writers' comradeship and compassion within the group. The first use of a word in Persian or Pashto is *italicised*, followed by an English translation; subsequent uses of a frequently used word are unitalicised. Often the italicised words are forms of address commonly used among the writers, such as *jan* (in Persian) or *jani* (in Pashto), dear; a term of endearment but also of respect for one another. The words for mother, *madar* in Persian or *mor* in Pashto, father, *padar*, and greetings, as *Salam*, appear throughout. I also retain the colloquial way of referring to a member of the Taliban as a Talib, as well as the plural form Taliba. At times, the writers mention titles of books they are reading in Persian translation; they are given their original titles in this book, as are the characters from world literature. As for the emojis embedded in the messages, I decided to leave them out because they were too specific and at the same time too generalised to convey anything close to what was being expressed in the moment.

The moment I joined this project I knew where I was heading. These writers were going to take me to places and describe situations I had not been in for a long time and would deepen the lasting pain and misery I have felt since the fall of Kabul. These are powerful voices who tell history from within. These women are not writing to be saved; this is their testimony. They are in this together, connected through the act of writing, and that's how *My Dear Kabul* is composed. Through my translation of their bravery, I have walked alongside them, observing the landscape of our country, collapsing helplessly on the face of the Earth, day by day, night after night. And I see that the only hope resides in these women's voices.

Parwana Fayyaz
Peterhouse, Cambridge University
January 2024

Acknowledgements

On behalf of Untold Narratives:

We could not have begun to put this book together without Arts Council England, who supported us using public funding from the National Lottery. We are grateful for the continued support of the Bagri Foundation and our private donors, who believe in the importance of our work.

Thank you to our Chair, Sarah Gardner, and co-director Bill Hicks for their faith in this project, along with the rest of the Untold team: Rachel Crome, Emma D'Costa, Sarah Miguel, Azadeh Parsapour, Katri Skala and Patrick Spaven. Also to Sharmilla Beezmohun, David Belton, Alexander Bodin Saphir, Antonia Byatt, Nicola Dahrendorf, James Greenshields, Mary Hockaday, Ross Holder, Marion Hume, Kawoon Khamoosh, Lucy Lyon, Prospero World, Rob Jago, Sally Thomas, Janie Wilson, Judith Witting and the many ambassadors for Untold's ongoing work.

We are grateful to those who published excerpts from this diary in its early stages, including in the *FT Weekend*. Excerpts also appeared in the BBC's *#100 Women* series, with thanks to Lyse Doucet and translator Dr Zubair Popalzai. This diary was also the inspiration for *Rising After the Fall* (Scholastic, 2023), co-edited by Lucy Hannah and Zarghuna Kargar.

A crucial thank you to Harriet Poland and the team at Coronet for their immediate interest in publishing the diary as a book and thanks to Hannah Black, Tom Atkins, and copy-editor Robina Pelham Burn for seeing it through to completion with such respect for the writers' words. Thanks also to proofreader Jacqui Lewis and map consultant Philip Parker. We are grateful to Untold Narratives' literary agent, Amy St Johnston at Aitken Alexander Associates, for being a constant support and sounding board. Our gratitude to Allia Popal for her patience and skill in interpreting our calls with the writers throughout the editing process. And to Clara Collyns for her ready help in the production process.

Thank you to Pashtana Durrani, always graciously ready to advise. Thanks also to Robert Chatterton-Dickson and Horia Mosadiq for their time, and to Deane Smith, who helps to keep these writers as safe as possible. We're also really grateful to those who read the book in manuscript form, among them Lin Coghlan, Sarala Emmanuel, Lucy Lethbridge, Aunohita Mojumdar, Samay Hamed, Suhrab Sirat and Gillian Slovo.

The editors would like to express their personal thanks to Kusal Perera, Kavan and Mithra Perera, Ghulam Sarwar Fayyaz, Roqea Fayyaz, Shabnam Fayyaz and Luca Zenobi.

Thanks, above all, to the writers who embarked on writing this diary, one day and message at a time. And to Will Forrester and Dr Negeen Kargar, who downloaded, stored and translated their messages over the course of a full year.

About Untold Narratives

Untold works to develop and amplify the work of writers marginalised by community or conflict. Its translators and editors work collaboratively with writers to develop their craft, connect them to one another and share their stories with readers in their local languages, and globally in translation.

Editors and translators of *My Dear Kabul*

Parwana Fayyaz is a scholar and teacher of Persian literature at the University of Cambridge. She is also a poet and translator working with multiple languages. Her poetry collection, *Forty Names* (Carcanet Press, 2021), was a *New Statesman* book of the year and a *White Review* book of the year. Her translations promote the writings and culture of Afghan people around the world.

Sunila Galappatti has worked with other people's stories as a dramaturg, theatre director, editor and writer: at the Royal Shakespeare Company, Live Theatre (Newcastle), Galle Literary Festival, Raking Leaves, Suriya Women's Development Centre, Commonwealth Writers, *Himal Southasian* and Untold Narratives. She spent five years working with a long-term prisoner of war in the Sri Lankan conflict, to retell his story in *A Long Watch* (Hurst, 2016).

Lucy Hannah is founder and director of Untold Narratives. A social entrepreneur, editor and author, she has worked with writers in the

UK and worldwide to develop and promote their work. Other initiatives Lucy has established include Commonwealth Writers, Out of the Gate and BBC Writers. She is a Visiting Research Fellow at King's College, London and a director of the Bocas Lit Fest in Trinidad.

Dr Negeen Kargar is a senior research scientist with a keen interest in literature and languages. She speaks Pashto, Dari, English, Urdu and German. She has worked as a translator for nearly twenty years and with this group of Afghan writers for Untold Narratives since 2019.

Lillie Razvi Toon works at the intersection between human rights and literature. She has worked for REDRESS, seeking justice for survivors of torture, and as an assistant producer at Wimbledon BookFest. She is the project manager at Untold Narratives.

Saturday 6 Sept

- Borrowed pen — need best of things from Frances — Sally

- Phone charger for phone

- payment details to transfer for William (Frances)

- parts — multiple pairs

- check flat — tidy bed — sitting room — wash up in kitchen — TIDY

- diary + pens for writing lovely calm mind —
Best I have been in — just 8 days — 8 days — all but 1 female —

Mix of care illness types + harder cases — Indian to my right English to my left My nurse is from Calcutta but trained in Edinburgh in haematol/oncol carefu...

wad 8 in the western for
Rebecca — lovely young
woman with IRISH Scottish boyfre.
Will put on my cotton
stripped night dress at
7.00 whi it is by a window-
dsn't sight of out doors all
day really — One But
later Socked — Oh
derch

Where is my bag
with debit + credit
cards? Is it on or
by the bed? probably

Where is my maroon
sparkly walking
stick with tassle?
important

where is my ipad and cover? -

It is 7.50 am and still dark outside — rather sad but calm inside — should pick up before too long?

$730 pm and still here — Sunday 6 Sept — going to western Gen ward 3 ASAP

will be OK but slow